STEPPING STONES:

The First Five Years of Sant Bani School

(1973-1978)

STEPPING STONES:

The First Five Years of Sant Bani School

(1973-1978)

The earlier days of school life are like the stepping stones to the building of a person's career.

Sant Ajaib Singh

Be Good. Do Good. Be One.

Master Kirpal Singh

Kent Bicknell

With Thanks

This history of the formative years of Sant Bani School is dedicated to everyone who had a part in creating and sustaining the school in the past, as well as those who will play such a role in the future. The school was built on the vision of two spiritual teachers from India, Master Kirpal Singh and Sant Ajaib Singh, and has thrived owing to the commitment of the many teachers, students, parents and friends who cared. May it continue to educate new generations of students steeped in core values that are timeless.

Cover photo: wall of the original Stone Building, built in 1973/4.
Inset photo: aerial view of SBS campus, 2017.

CONTENTS

Introduction: Under a Double Rainbow

WANTED
Large isolated farmhouse
Far from traffic and neighbors

The first hint of what grew into Sant Bani School (SBS)[1] lay in the vision of a young couple, Russell and Judith Perkins, who in the early 1960s dreamed of living quietly and raising their children among fields and forests rather than cities or suburbs. As Russell grew up in Sanbornton, New Hampshire, they chose to look in the Lakes Region of central New Hampshire, eventually placing a classified advertisement in the *Laconia Citizen* with the above headline.

In September of 1962 they purchased an abandoned dairy farm of over 200 acres on which stood a colonial house built in the late 1700s and a smaller house built in the 1930s. They called their new home "Sant Bani Farm," in honor of the spiritual teacher from India they were following, Master Kirpal Singh (1894-1974). "Sant Bani" is from the Sanskrit, and while I like to translate it as "Song of the Spirit," it can have multiple meanings.[2]

When Master Kirpal toured the United States in 1963 Russell and Judith invited him to come to their home, which he did on October 11, 1963. That evening he gave a talk at the Unitarian Church in Franklin, New Hampshire, during which he called the Perkins's place "Sant Bani Ashram" rather than "Sant Bani Farm." At that moment Judith and Russell understood that their isolated lifestyle was quite likely to change as an *ashram* is a retreat center dedicated to the practice of a spiritual path. As Master Kirpal explained to

---

[1] For the first decade the school was called "Sant Bani Ashram School," as it was founded on ashram grounds and was overseen by the board of directors of Sant Bani Ashram, Inc. In 1983 Sant Ajaib Singh advised that the school and ashram become separate entities (see Chapter VI). At that time he endorsed calling the school "Sant Bani School" instead. Rather than change the name mid-stream, I use the terms "Sant Bani School" and "SBS" to refer to the school throughout this book.
[2] In Sanskrit *Sant* translates best as saintly, holy or of the spirit, and *Bani* as hymn, celestial song or "the Word:" the life current running through all living things.

1

Russell once, "*Sant Bani Ashram* means, 'Where the teachings of the Masters are put to work'."

The 1960s witnessed a blossoming that soon became an explosion of young people turning to the Asian Wisdom Traditions to satisfy their hunger for a more spiritual life. Sant Bani Ashram was very much in the thick of this movement as more and more people visited to find out what Master Kirpal Singh and the teachings known as *Sant Mat* had to offer.[3] Many who came to visit had children (or soon would), so the idea of starting a school to support a value system different than the predominant culture made a lot of sense. As Russell shared with school parents in 2001, "Judith and I always assumed we would have a school here someday. We both had difficult experiences in public schools and wanted something better for our children."

Karen and I first visited Sant Bani Ashram in March of 1968. We were very drawn to the spiritual path taught by Master Kirpal Singh and so became *Satsangis*[4] when we were initiated into Sant Mat in May of that year. At a time when a number of my friends suggested I do something practical like attend a trade school or learn a craft, Judith and Russell encouraged me to go back to college to be better prepared to start a school. I did, and graduated from Yale University in 1970.

In the meantime, Russell and Judith discovered Horizon's Edge School, a wonderful progressive elementary school located in Canterbury, New Hampshire, about half an hour from Sant Bani

---

[3] Sant Mat teaches that God (above gender) exists and manifests through the vibrational forces of light and sound. A Guru or Master is someone who has connected with that light and sound within and has reached God-consciousness by following those twin streams back to their source. Further, the Guru can help others do the same. Little outer change is required beyond adopting a vegetarian diet free of all intoxicants and earning one's livelihood through honest means. The real challenge is the daily inner work: stilling the mind to be able to catch hold of the traces of the inner light and sound through specific meditation practices. As explained in Chapter IV, SBS decided early on that it was not appropriate for teachers to be instructing students in the very specific meditation practices associated with the ashram.

[4] "Satsangi" is the term that will be used to designate an initiate of the Masters in the spiritual Path of Sant Mat that is followed at Sant Bani Ashram and elsewhere. *Sat* means "truth" and *sangi* means "someone who is connected with..." Services at Sant Bani Ashram are called "Satsangs," and the main building for meditation is called the "Satsang Hall."

Ashram. Their older child, Miriam, attended, as did their son Eric when he was ready for school.[5] Judith began to work at Horizon's Edge alongside the founders, Bill Meeh and his extraordinary wife, Mildred, who was to have an enormous influence on SBS.

With the growth of the ashram community[6] the idea of starting a school began to take shape. By the spring of 1973 there were three local Satsangi families with children who wished to have a school in harmony with the teachings of Master Kirpal as well as another family who moved to the area to be close to the ashram. A particular concern for Satsangi families at the time was how a vegetarian diet would be received in the public schools. To those of us who embraced Sant Mat as a way of life, the choice to live on a plant-based diet made perfect sense, not only spiritually, ethically and physically but also to lessen the strain on earth's limited resources. We did not want our children to feel abnormal or somehow less because they were vegetarian.[7] At the same time we wanted them to develop their hearts and minds as well as participate in music,

---

[5] It is interesting to note that a school was housed temporarily on the ashram prior to Sant Bani School. In the fall of 1968 Helen Ryan, a friend of the Perkinses, founded Heart Hill School. As her home in Northfield was not ready the school opened in the Big House, the 200-year-old colonial farmhouse at the ashram. Miriam and Eric tried Heart Hill for a year but were happy to return to their much-loved Horizon's Edge.

[6] What is meant by "the growth of the ashram community" is that the number of people in the area who were connected to the ashram increased, either because local people came to Sant Mat or people from afar relocated in the Lakes Region of New Hampshire to be closer to the ashram, but not live on it. The ashram was never intended to be a place where people could live in isolation and the retreats it continues to host allow guests to immerse themselves in an intense schedule of meditation for a few days to a week. From the beginning, the only people who resided on the premises were the voluntary staff who maintain it for the benefit of others.

[7] The vegetarian diet on campus and at all school-sponsored events continues to be an essential commitment/core operating principle of SBS today: *"The School's neighbor, Sant Bani Ashram, was established as a sanctuary for living creatures, and, beyond the obvious restrictions against hunting and fishing, there is also the practice of respecting all life through a vegetarian diet. This diet, a means to cause us little harm as possible, is practiced in the School as well. While students and families are not asked to change their diets outside of school, it is required that all food brought to and consumed on campus, or as part of any school function, be vegetarian and egg-free."* (2016-17 Parent-Student Handbook, p. 33).

3

art, sports, drama and, especially, to understand the value of service to others.

As momentum for a school grew, Russell and Judith asked me if I would be principal. At the same time they asked Mildred Meeh if she would be an advisor. Although I had a great position as one of two Child Care Consultants for the State of New Hampshire, I eagerly said, "Yes!" Mildred, who was teaching full-time as well as running Horizon's Edge School, also graciously agreed. Before moving forward with such an important undertaking Russell wrote to Master Kirpal for advice. In his March 1973 letter Russell explained that there were people who wished to have a school that would support Satsangi values and mentioned that both Mildred and I were willing to be involved.

In May the response we had been anxiously awaiting arrived from India. Russell and Judith brought the letter across the field to the home Karen and I built on the ashram in 1970. We were all very happy that Master Kirpal endorsed the founding of a school at Sant Bani. As we sat in our small living room (soon to become the first classroom) we became almost giddy as we read the good news over and over again. When the four of us stepped into our front yard we saw a brilliant double rainbow arching across the southern sky from Franklin to what would become the main campus of Sant Bani School. We took it as a sign and were ready to begin.

When word got out that Sant Bani Ashram was founding a school a number of pieces came together. Our enrollment went from four students to five when another Satsangi family moved from New York so their son could begin first grade with us. As the summer rolled on we were delighted to receive an inquiry from a family who was not connected to the ashram. They were looking for something other than the local public school for their son, and my mother (a highly-respected teacher in the elementary school the boy attended) recommended they consider SBS, which had just been approved by the State of New Hampshire. They did, and we were thrilled to have him join us as a fifth grader given that it had always been our intention to create a school that would reach beyond the Satsangi community to any family seeking a positive educational experience. To convert others to our way of life was never a goal; our idea was to build a great school that would do all the things any school should do while supporting our values.[8]

With enrollment now at six students a second positive development came into play. Tibor Farkas, a Canadian Satsangi who had recently graduated from architecture school, agreed to design and oversee the construction of the building. Using the majestic clerestory approach with lots of windows, Tibor drew up plans that honored the contours of the voluminous ledge we uncovered on the designated spot (right behind the Bicknell house). The split-level building included a large room on the upper level with a small office and two bathrooms on a level below, all heated by a central wood stove and radiant floor heat. We chose to use local field stones for the outer walls, following the system developed by Helen and Scott Nearing as outlined in their 1954 classic, *Living the Good Life: How to Live Simply and Sanely in a Troubled World*. Given that the work force for construction was all volunteers it is no surprise that the original Stone Building was not ready until the following year. Undeterred, volunteers helped Karen and me prepare our home for the beginning of the school year.

So it was that on Monday the 10th of September, 1973, SBS opened its (only) door with six fearless students and one teacher (me!). The "original six" were:

- Beverly and Ben (Grade 1)
- Thomas (Grade 2)
- Joey (Grade 3)
- Peter (Grade 5)
- Eric (Grade 7)

****

---

[8] Master Kirpal made this quite clear to us in a number of ways. In a wonderful message he penned called "Ends and Means," he pointed out how too often the means for achieving something can be taken as the goal itself: *"It is very necessary to distinguish clearly the ends from the means. To lay too much stress on the means is likely to make us gradually forget our objective and to become fossilized. Once we know, for example, that abstinence from all kinds of meat diet and spirituous liquors helps us on the spiritual Path, it is enough that we avoid them. But to take it as an end in itself is to miss the goal. Offending others because they eat meat is worse than meat eating itself."* (Circular Letter #3, November 22, 1956) http://www.ruhanisatsangusa.org/means.htm).

Richmond Mayo-Smith, a beloved trustee of SBS with broad and deep educational experience,[9] once asked me about the roots of the school. He wrote, *"To my memory the Board of Trustees has never heard you talk about what you had in mind when you set forth creating Sant Bani School. What key learning experiences shaped the growth of the school? I think this would be worth knowing as from some source you seem to have gained ideas which are now being recognized by leading experts."*[10] The chapters in this book delineate key learning experiences that shaped pedagogy in the school's formative years as they sketch a picture of day-to-day life from 1973 through 1978.

---

[9] Richmond (1922-2015) served on the boards of numerous humanitarian, service and education organizations including Sant Bani School for many years; two of his grandchildren graduated from SBS. After teaching science for fifteen years at Phillips Exeter Academy he became Head of Roxbury Latin School for eight years. He worked in India for three and a half years in community development with the organization World Education Inc. He was also one of the co-founders of Educators for Social Responsibility and served as its chair. He served on the boards of the Marion Foundation, World Education, Center Heart and Sant Bani School. He also served as chair of the board for the Center for Psychology & Social Change.
[10] Email from Richmond Mayo-Smith to Kent Bicknell on May 11, 2006.

Chapter I: The First Year (1973-74)

The very nature of education has to be transformed so that it can give society young men and women who are not only intellectually but emotionally trained for vigorous, realistic and constructive leadership.

Master Kirpal Singh

Toward the New Education

In the late 1960s Master Kirpal Singh chose a beautiful spot in the foothills of the Himalayas to begin building *Manav Kendra* (Center for Humanity), a complex that would come to include a home for elders, a medical center, a dairy farm, vegetable and flower gardens, a library with books on religions of the world, a meditation center with a large reflective pool and a school to serve local children who otherwise would have had no opportunity for an education.

On June 21, 1972, Master Kirpal presided over the opening ceremonies of the school, *Manav Vidya Mandir* (Temple of Human Knowledge). His keynote address, "Toward the New Education,"[11] quickly became a founding document for Sant Bani School as it is filled with guidance that we took to heart. To capture a sense of the address, here are some excerpts:

- The most important thing about education is its relation to life. "Knowledge without action is empty as a shadow."
- The school should be a home of teachers and students who reflect in their studies, and on the playground and in their daily lives, the cherished virtue of humility. Till our knowledge enables us to imbibe the noblest things of life, it has not served its purpose. Al-Ghazali, a man of scholarship and meditation, says in his book *Child*, "Know, my child, that knowledge without action is insanity, and the noblest action is service."

---

[11] See Appendix.

- The chief malady of current education is that it results in the disassociation of heart and head. It lays emphasis on the development of head, and does sharpen the intellect to some extent. But more essential is the liberation of the heart. That will be done when the reason is awakened in sympathy for the poor, the weak and the needy.
- It is the proper atmosphere which can deliver the goods; that is why emphasis in the school should be on atmosphere more than on rules, textbooks and buildings.
- The tender heart of a child calls for very delicate handling. In fact, education begins even before birth and therefore better care must be bestowed upon every pregnant mother. It is a constant association with gentle forces which breeds virtuous persons. A child is the center of creative life and needs to be opened as a flower is opened, gently, by sympathy, not by force. Do not let the child be imprisoned in the examination machine; never let him be snubbed and scolded.
- It is a lamentable fact that present education, which should insure an integrated growth of human personality, provides a very incomplete and insufficient preparation for life.
- In this process, the situation of the school also plays a major role. The German word *kindergarten* is quite suggestive in this context. *Kinder* means child, and *garten* garden, indicating that every school should be situated in a lovely spot of nature.
- The institution is dedicated to the concrete realization of human unity and is projected as an entirely new concept of integral education and moral living according to the ethics of spirituality.
- To accomplish this vital and indispensable task, the very nature of education has to be transformed so that it can give society young men and women who are not only intellectually but emotionally trained for vigorous, realistic and constructive leadership. We envisage such an atmosphere where persons will be able to grow and develop integrally without losing contact with their souls.

The above was the charge, and in the initial years of Sant Bani School there were a number of key people who helped lay the foundation for what SBS was to become through putting this charge into practice. The influence of others will be discussed in subsequent chapters; the first year, however, began with me.

What I Brought to Sant Bani School

It seemed that education was in my blood. Not only were both my parents teachers but in the 1950s we lived on the campuses of different independent schools. While we returned to New Hampshire every summer, the school year was spent teaching at Chadwick School in Los Angeles, followed by Southern Arizona School in Tucson. As I was entering fifth grade we came back to New Hampshire for good when my father, Lansing L. Bicknell, returned to teach at New Hampton School where his career began in 1937. My mother, Ruth G. Bicknell, taught in the primary grades at Lang Street School in Meredith for several years before transferring to the New Hampton Community School.

What I remember most from those early years was the strength of my family. Though my brothers and I fought at times, mostly we had lots of fun, especially driving our parents crazy with puns at the dinner table. Whether I was at school, in the dining hall, in the dormitory,[12] exploring the surrounding woods and streams, or on the tennis courts, I always felt the love and support of my parents.[13]

When I got old enough to reflect on my early childhood I understood how lucky I had been to grow up on a secure and beautiful campus surrounded by forests, rivers and hills, all of which my friends and I could access at a moment's notice. [14]

_____

[12] When we were in grade school Stuart and I shared a small dorm room surrounded by 10th grade boys that was downstairs from my parents' faculty apartment.

[13] Example: when I was five years old my father and I developed a game. As we walked along a city street in Tucson he would hold my small hand in his. When he gently squeezed once, I would turn my hand into a fist, which he continued to hold. After a while (the time varied) he would give my fist two soft squeezes and I would open it up to hold his hand "normally" once again. We would continue playing this as we walked along. The amazing thing is that we never said one word about it; it naturally developed and became something we both looked forward to. On another note, my mother saved a lot of my artwork and creative writing from my youngest years, giving me the message that what I did was worthwhile. As I look at these pieces today I am grateful for her efforts on my behalf.

[14] I had an inkling of self-reflection (my first "Ah-ha" moment perhaps) when I was sitting on a bench in front of the house I now call home. I was twelve years old and my friends and I enjoyed watching the summer traffic crawl through the center of quiet New Hampton Village as, prior to the completion of Interstate 93, Main Street was part of the direct route to the White Mountains. When my family

When I was thirteen I ran a summer camp for the children of our neighbors on Murray Hill Road in Hill, New Hampshire. As all their names began with a "K" we called it "Kent Kamp!" Three days a week we sketched and painted, constructed wooden gizmos, made our own playdough, practiced archery, learned to box, performed magic tricks, read, took nature walks, picked blueberries, acted, and played cards, croquet, ping pong and badminton. While I passed along "skills" taught me by my two older brothers we all had fun.

In the 1950s and '60s New Hampton was an all-boys "prep" school, a solid link in the chain of traditional New England boarding schools. As my father was a history teacher, coach and athletic director and my mother a highly regarded 2nd and 3rd grade teacher in the local public schools, it perhaps is not a surprise that I worked hard at my studies and loved sports.

The quality of the faculty was high and I learned a great deal. While there is much I could share about those four years a moment that has always stood out for me was when my 10th grade Geometry class sat for our end-of-year final exam. Our teacher, Skip Howard, handed out the exam (and the requisite "blue book") and noted that it consisted of five of the most challenging problems in geometry he could find. He let us look them over and then shared that as he was only interested in seeing what each of us could do with them, the whole exam was optional. He explained that he had already given us our final grades as he knew the quality of work each student had done over the year. After noting that we were free to leave and that it would not affect our grade if we chose not to tackle the problems, he left us on our own. We were dumbfounded, and we

---

and I were driving from Arizona to New Hampshire twice a year I had the habit of looking out the window at children in the towns we went through and thinking, "I am so much luckier than those kids who are stuck in this town. I get to be driving across the country." As I sat on the bench watching yet another car go slowly by, I saw a child peering at me from the window. Instantly I thought, "Look at that poor kid, stuck in that car while I am so lucky to be living here in New Hampton." I immediately caught the irony of my thinking and burst out laughing. When a friend asked me what was up I tried to explain that I had just seen how I view everything from my own perspective—and then, selfishly, think that is best. While I struggled at the time to find the words to convey the impact, the truth of that moment—of my sudden realization of how self-centered I could be—never left me.

all chose to sit there for the required two hours and do our best to solve those geometric mysteries. I was moved by the powerful pedagogy of an adult who was hungry to know what I thought, who trusted me completely and who knew me so well that a final exam was superfluous.

A couple of weeks after graduating from New Hampton[15] I shipped out of Montreal on an old freighter with a school friend, Erik Hvoslef, and headed across the Atlantic to Norway. Living in the city of Oslo with Erik's uncle, we worked for a few weeks in a government bottling plant prior to spending time in a summer cottage on Oslo Fjord. While initially grousing how terrible it was that the "socialist government" took half of our weekly pay, Erik and I began to notice all the services available like health care for all and free passage for elders on public transportation. Most striking of all was the absence of huge economic gaps among Norwegians.

In our time on Oslo Fjord our host, an attorney about to send his son to New Hampton, explained to us that he earned $10,000 a year and was taxed $4000, leaving him $6000 to live on. This was enough for a nice house in Oslo as well as a summer house on the water. The nearby fishermen were making about $2000 a year and were subsidized another $2000 from taxes. This meant that the fishermen's families had only $2000 less a year to live on than his family, and he was very happy to share his income to lessen the disparity. During evening conversations, he asked us challenging questions such as why the United States was getting more engaged in Vietnam, and how come our country spent so little on education compared to, for example, the Scandinavian countries. As neither Erik nor I knew enough to respond well, we ended up questioning the value of what we had learned in school. While loving the beauty of the fjord we were exhausted by the nightly grilling and were happy to rent a car so we could experience more of the natural beauty of Norway.

In so many ways this was an eye-opening journey for an 18-year-old. I recall that on the flight back to America I wondered, for the first time, what it might be like to settle and live in a country other than the United States. Were there, in fact, alternate places

---

[15] June 6, 1965.

and/or ways to live that might be an improvement on what I saw in my native country?

In September I headed to Yale University in New Haven, Connecticut. I had not been on the campus until my parents dropped me off a couple of days before classes began. I plunged into all the normal first-year courses and played on the freshman soccer team. Toward the middle of the year I started to explore alternate ways of approaching the mystery called "life." This was prime time for a generation that, as it came of age, was eager to push boundaries in its restlessness to find the full extent of what life had to offer. In our hearts we knew that there had to be more than had been presented to us thus far.

After a summer divided between working with children in the Dwight Street Projects of New Haven and living with friends in an apartment on River Street in Cambridge, Massachusetts, I entered sophomore year seriously wondering what might lie beyond the horizon of "the American Dream."[16] To broaden my perspective I enrolled in *Religious Studies 34a*, a seminar in modern Hinduism where we studied in depth the lives of four colossal figures of nineteenth and twentieth century India: Sri Ramakrishna, Ramana Maharshi, Rabindranath Tagore, and Mahatma Gandhi.[17]

The professor, Dr. Norvin Hein, was a scholar who approached each student like he did the historical giants in the course: as if we mattered. As a burgeoning hippy with an awakening consciousness, I was thrilled to read about these lofty figures. When I saw the black and white photo of the Indian saint Sri Ramakrishna so completely lost in *samadhi* (God-intoxication) that his disciples had to support him by the elbows, I was thunderstruck. As I stared at the photo taken September 21, 1879, I thought, "Wow! This saint was alive when my grandfather was a boy!" I understood at that moment that saints not only existed 2000 years ago but recently as well—which meant that somewhere a saint might be alive in 1966.

In the midst of my awakening sense of spiritual possibilities, I wrote incredibly enthusiastic papers for Professor Hein. This kind

---

[16] Which, in our youthful exuberance, we summed up as "a better job, a bigger house, and two (or three!) cars in the garage…"

[17] From the Yale College course catalogue: "*Religious Studies 34a, Modern Hinduism.* A study of the creative Hindu religious leaders of the nineteenth and twentieth centuries, with special attention to types of religious experiences."

and tolerant professor in no way belittled my far-reaching papers; he in no way advised me to stick to safe scholarly analysis. On the contrary, he was supportive of my search, took it as real, and thereby validated my growing hunger for more knowledge about the spiritual life. In his plain brown suit, wire-rim glasses and humble demeanor, Professor Hein honored the birth of a quest in my heart. By appreciating my writing as "showing the priceless ingredient of courage to tackle a problem head-on,"[18] he strengthened my resolve to search for a spiritual path.

Along with the seminar in modern Hinduism I took a course in Chinese literature (in translation). The inner flame was fanned as I read through the many poems from *Cold Mountain*, written by a Zen Buddhist who, one thousand years before, stepped away from worldly pursuits to seek inner knowledge. With a couple of other students I petitioned to live off-campus, a choice previously reserved for married students. At a requisite meeting with the well-known head of the housing quad where I lived, Thomas Bergin, I was informed that if I were allowed to follow my plan I would "miss out on the true-Blue experience of Yale." I acknowledged the accuracy of his observation and responded that perhaps I was looking for something else. Yale College granted our petition and we moved to a beach house in East Haven.

In the next few months I concluded that being a university student was neither what I wanted or needed at that point in my life.[19] With the Rolling Stones' "Ruby Tuesday" whispering in my ear to *"Catch your dreams before they slip away"* and visions of a utopian community dancing in my head, I dropped out of Yale in the spring of 1967 with Michael Folz, a close friend who was a brilliant songwriter. Our goal was to create good music, make a lot of money, and then move to the Canadian Rockies to build a community where we could live in peace and harmony. We moved to NYC to start a band with some students at Columbia University.

---

[18] Written comment by Professor Hein on my paper, "Correlations of Sri Ramakrishna, Psychoses, and LSD" handed in on November 2, 1966.

[19] Given my long hair and bell-bottoms (one of a handful of students who looked like that in late '66) I received mixed support at Yale: very positive from the professors yet openly hostile from many of the students as I was yelled at, sworn at, spat at, ridiculed, etc. When I returned as a married student in the fall of '68 everything had changed as the '60s look was in full bloom on campus.

After a few weeks we had very little music to show for our efforts[20] and, fed up with sleeping on dormitory floors, we decided to hitchhike west. Our goal was to find the next area in the country that would explode in "hipness" as had happened in San Francisco, become a top local band there, and get launched to stardom like *Jefferson Airplane* and *The Grateful Dead.* Following a variety of adventures with assorted characters in Minneapolis, Kansas City, Reno, Sparks, Denver, the Grand Canyon, Oak Creek Canyon, San Francisco, and Denver again, we decided that the Denver/Boulder area would be the new mecca. I had classmates from New Hampton who were at the University of Denver (DU) and the University of Colorado-Boulder, so there were more floors we could sleep on. After a short time Michael headed east to gather the other members of the band while I stayed with a friend from New Hampton who was attending DU.

On my twentieth birthday, May 13, 1967, I checked in with my parents who told me that my cousin had been killed in Vietnam, a very sad reminder of the current state of the world. I reflected long and hard on how my search for a more meaningful way of life related to the sacrifice my cousin made. I found no easy answers but understood I had to continue my quest. As a good friend of mine observed, our generation was "eager to move beyond the boundaries of our inherited culture,"[21] and I was "all in."

Exactly one week later, my friend and I were shopping for groceries when he said hello to a young woman across the aisle. I inquired, "Who is that?" and he responded that she was a casual acquaintance named Karen Hawkinson. I asked him to introduce us, which he did. It turned out that Karen had been wondering who I was and within a very short time we were inseparable. She was a sophomore at DU but decided to stay with me rather than return to her home in Minneapolis for the summer. As none of the Columbia University musicians were willing to leave NYC, the dream of becoming the best rock band in the Denver/Boulder area quickly faded and Karen and I decided to head back to New England.

---

[20] An exception was a rendition of John Keats' "Ode to a Nightingale" set to a stirring arrangement that rose in a crescendo that rang out, "Truth is beauty – beauty truth" over and over again. Our lead guitar player was Chris Donald who went on to play for the "doo-wop" revival group, Sha Na Na.
[21] Thanks to Don Macken for this great phrasing.

We returned to New Hampshire to live with my parents and were married on my father's birthday, September 4, 1967. I was now a college drop-out, married, and had no gainful employment. Initially Karen took a job at the Laconia Dunkin' Donuts and I became a night watchman for New Hampton School, and in the winter we moved on to work at Loon Mountain Ski Area. As we were still hungry to find a more meaningful way of life we avidly studied various spiritual movements. A long-time faculty member at New Hampton, Dave Rice, heard of our interest and suggested we might want to visit Sant Bani Ashram in the neighboring town of Sanbornton. This news came as such a surprise as I had no idea there was an ashram anywhere near where I grew up.

Mr. Rice wrote out directions for us and on a lovely March day in 1968 we were off to explore in my brother's Volkswagen "tomato" bug. After driving for a long time up a narrow dirt road[22] we came to a simple wooden sign that said in big letters:

> ## WELCOME
> ## TO
> ## SANT BANI ASHRAM
> *
> ## Please don't kill our neighbors,
> ## the birds, fish and animals

Expecting pagoda-shaped buildings and monks in saffron robes, we knocked on the front door of the Big House, a 200-year-old colonial building. An elderly man with flowing hair and a long white beard opened the door and, with twinkling eyes and a gentle voice, welcomed us to Sant Bani Ashram. This was Gerald Boyce, a native of Franklin, New Hampshire, who had traveled around the country decades earlier on his own quest. After meeting Master Kirpal during his visit to New Hampshire in 1963[23] Gerald decided that what he had been looking for all his life had come to him. Another elder, Betty Shifflett, made organic peanut butter sandwiches

---

[22] Osgood Road used to be a mile and a half of dirt road, especially challenging in mud season!
[23] See Introduction.

15

for us on home-made whole wheat bread and served us herbal tea. We were invited to ask as many questions as we liked, and after a couple of hours we left with a small amount of literature on Sant Mat and almost all our questions answered.

While we did not meet Russell and Judith Perkins at that time we soon learned that Jim Cluett, a friend from New Hampton School, had just returned from a six month stay in India with Master Kirpal. As Jim was on his way to Florida, Karen and I decided to hitchhike down the East Coast and connect with him in Fort Lauderdale. Along the way we wanted to visit a few other centers of spirituality as our interest had been piqued. Shortly before we left New Hampton my father took Karen aside and asked if she really wanted to embark on this trip or was it something she was doing because she loved me. When she responded that she really wanted to go, he confided, "Well, secretly I really admire you both!" As had been the case from earliest childhood I felt the support of my parents as we set out on our journey.

Hitchhiking south we stopped for a couple days at the Vedanta Center in Cohasset, Massachusetts, founded by Swami Vivekananda in the late 1800s. We knew of Swami Vivekananda's extensive early work in the 1890s in Chicago, New York, Boston and San Francisco through our study of Sri Ramakrishna, Vivekananda's spiritual teacher. As we had been reading the works of Edgar Cayce, a well-known psychic who became famous for his healing work in the first half of the 20th century, next up was the Edgar Cayce research center in Virginia Beach, Virginia.[24]

We arrived in Florida and after more study and conversation with initiates of Master Kirpal we decided that Sant Mat was just what we had been searching for. We were initiated on May 20, 1968, exactly one year after we met in Denver. For the first time since dropping out of college I could now envision returning to Yale. As mentioned above, Judith and Russell encouraged me to do this as it would be good preparation for starting a school. "Mother Yale" was very forgiving and welcomed me back with open arms. Karen and I rented an apartment on Dwight Street and I enrolled in classes for the fall of 1968.

---

[24] The Edgar Cayce center is called the Association for Research and Enlightenment, or A.R.E.

I spent the first year immersed in Spanish literature and in the spring applied to be a Scholar of the House, a special program that allowed a student to focus on one project the entire senior year. My goal was to study the esoteric writings of two 14th century English mystics, Walter Hilton and the anonymous author of *The Cloud of Unknowing*, through the lens of the writings of the 16th century Spanish mystic San Juan de la Cruz (St. John of the Cross). Accepted into the program I squirreled myself away in the chauffeur's quarters of an old estate in Woodbridge, Connecticut, just outside New Haven and read and wrote, read and wrote.[25]

A very exciting event happened in that we welcomed our son Christopher in January of 1970. Now approaching graduation, I knew I needed to find meaningful work and doubted there was much demand for someone well-versed in 500-year-old Christian mystical practices. Even though I had always enjoyed working with children, I was not eager to enroll in a certification program requiring a series of courses. During my time in Yale's Sterling Memorial Library I got to know some librarians who recommended I become a children's librarian. Shortly after commencement I enrolled in Columbia University's School of Library Science but stayed only a few days as I found the daily commute from rural Woodbridge to New York City to be too much.

Russell and Judith invited Karen and me to build a house on Sant Bani Ashram, so we moved to Sanbornton in the summer of 1970. I was hired by Merrimack Valley Child Care Center in Concord, New Hampshire, to be assistant teacher for the four-year-olds. Over the next two years I advanced to head teacher and then program director while I earned an M.A. in Early Childhood Education through a non-resident program at Goddard College in Vermont.

The research for my Master's degree examined ways to provide emotionally healthy environments for child care facilities. Too often the prevailing mode was a kindergarten model designed to "socialize" students who came in for half-days a few days a week. Child

---

[25] My Scholar of the House thesis, *The Ascent to God*, is available on request. My advisors were the renowned professors Jaroslav Pelikan and A. Bartlett Giamatti. Dr. Giamatti went on to become President of Yale, and then Commissioner of Major League Baseball.

care centers had very young children who needed to spend the entire day there and what made sense was to create a program that would allow them the kind of freedom and choice they would have if they were at home. Dr. Millie Penhale, the child psychologist who served as my consultant throughout the degree program, helped me focus on how best to meet the spatial needs of young children. In the end we designed several large-scale moveable indoor structures that allowed the children the freedom to simply "be" without feeling that adults were constantly hovering. At the same time staff felt very comfortable that the children, though not always in sight, were safe. Through this work I gained an understanding of how important it is for children to have lots of opportunities to explore, to learn and to be on their own rather than be driven by a rigid schedule of Playdough at 10:15, Snacks at 11, and Outside Recess from 11:15 to 11:30. A critical experience in my two years at Merrimack Valley Child Care Center was the daily reminder of how much I enjoyed working with children!

Following Merrimack Valley I was hired to be a Child Care Consultant for the State of New Hampshire. My duties included traveling around the state to help start-ups, working with social workers and legislators on how best to regulate child care facilities, selecting four distinct programs to be filmed as models for diverse approaches to nurturing environments for young children and trouble-shooting issues that came up as more child care centers came into being. While most aspects of this role were informative and interesting I rarely had a chance to work with children directly, which I sorely missed. Once the plan to start Sant Bani School had wings[26] I jumped at the opportunity.

Preparing for the Opening of Sant Bani School

Recognizing that my background was in early childhood education rather than elementary school instruction, I sought training to be as prepared as possible for teaching six students spanning grades 1-7. My natural inclination was to adopt a child-centered approach and I gravitated to a curricular model known as "the British Infant System." The core curriculum was built around the child's

---

[26] See Introduction.

18

natural curiosity, and a classroom was set up with various stations filled with manipulative materials and a number of directed problems that the students could work to solve, individually or as a group. The teacher served more as a facilitator/coach than a repository of knowledge, with a "learning through play" pedagogy drawn from the works of educators like Johann Pestalozzi, Bronson Alcott, Frederick Froebel, Maria Montessori, John Dewey and Jean Piaget.[27]

Over the summer I attended a workshop on the British Infant System held in Dublin, New Hampshire. I came back filled with enthusiasm for setting up math, science, social studies and language arts "activity stations" in our home. I ordered the requisite materials to outfit the classroom, including Cuisenaire rods, Unifix cubes, scales, magnets, pencil, paper, paints and brushes along with the Ladybird series of books published in England. These were a collection of small, thin books that were relatively easy to read and presented much information on diverse topics. I was initially amused by the alternate perspective offered by books written in another country but also saw their value as examples of bias, in ourselves and in others. It was fascinating, for example, to read the Ladybird book on electricity and find that the British scientist Michael Faraday was the key player in its discovery while Benjamin Franklin and Thomas Edison were relegated to a paragraph or two.[28]

---

[27] See, for example, http://education.stateuniversity.com/pages/2086/Infant-Schools-in-England.html

[28] A recent exhibit (March 2017) in the UK noted that many of the 1960s Ladybird books' illustrated science experiments would be "banned by today's health and safety brigade." The article concludes with a statement by Dr. Lawrence Zeegen, professor of Illustration and Dean of the School of Design at London College of Communications and co-curator of the Ladybird by Design exhibition: "*In the 1960s, health and safety was the last thing on anyone's mind, but there is no way children would be allowed to do these things today. The images reflect a time in recent history where children weren't mollycoddled or tracked on Facebook, they were allowed to play and explore and discover things for themselves. The experiments were things children could have a bash at and the fact there was no parent or teacher present added to the excitement. They were not wholly dangerous but there was certainly no consideration for health and safety. It is completely removed from today, where everything has to be risk-assessed. The pictures present an idyllic childhood in which children enjoyed adventures, long summer holidays and lots of independence. You were encouraged to explore, have adventures and do experiments. The images represent freedom in childhood, which children don't have so much today.*" http://www.telegraph.co.uk/news/newstopics/howaboutthat/11359517/Ladybird-books-from-the-1960s-that-would-be-banned-by-todays-

As further preparation for the September opening, Judith and Russell encouraged me to consult with Mildred Meeh, who had been approved as the school's adviser by Master Kirpal Singh. I spoke at length to Mildred about my philosophy and how I envisioned educational activities playing out on a daily basis. With her wealth of practically tempered experience she was concerned about whether students would really learn effectively via the British Infant System and shared her reservations with Judith and Russell. It was then proposed that Mildred function as a "superintendent" over my role as teaching-principal for the six students.

I proceeded to consult some with Mildred, implementing suggestions such as establishing benchmarks for spelling proficiency through administration of the Morrison-McCall spelling pre-test in September and adapting the Horizon's Edge daily schedule for SBS. For the most part, however, I avoided her and chose to go ahead on my own. Rather than embrace all that Mildred had to offer I felt threatened by this consummate professional who, once I got to know her, had so much to give in a unique, gentle, compassionate manner filled with grace.

The First Half of Year One

With the excitement building in students and parents alike, opening day, September 10, came at last. Parents dropped off their children, Ben and Beverly (1st), Thomas (2nd), Joey (3rd), Peter (5th) and Eric (7th) and they filled our small house. The students and I spent time going over essential elements of our 8:30AM to 3PM day. I explained that during class time I would be working with groups or individuals while others would be engaged at one of the several activity stations set up in our 13' by 15' living room. They would be learning about/working on reading and writing, math and problem solving, telling time, art and music, all in a setting conducive to the growth of the spirit.

---

health-and-safety-brigade.html. Looking over the small archive that remains of the original SBS Ladybird books there is no doubt they are dated: the 1965 book on how a "motor car" works begins, "Here is a book which all boys will find fascinating..."

Kent with the "original six" students on September 17, 1973

Language arts with the two 1st graders would happen from 9 to 10:15 while the four 2nd through 7th graders would work independently at the math station. After a short recess the 1st graders would work at the math station and language arts would happen for the other four from 10:30 to 11:30+. Following lunch and recess all the students would engage with either social studies or science until 2, and then it would be art, music and/or games until dismissal at 3.

I went over basic "housekeeping" rules including keeping the equipment and supplies neat and cleaning up after they finished. I stressed respect for each other and that, with different groups working on different things in a small space, it would be best to work quietly. I added that there would be plenty of time for recess which would include free play, various forms of tag, "Red Light/ Green Light," swinging on the rope swing out back of our home and helping build the Stone Building. From the beginning I stressed that there should be no fighting or play involving sticks as guns, etc. [29]

Each day we would begin with a period of quiet reflection, and then an extended reading (which quickly became known as "Morning Session"). During the first few weeks the students and I would sit quietly for about fifteen minutes, and then I would read from

---

[29] Much of this material is from a spiral-bound notebook that has my notes on the opening days of SBS.

21

The Lion, the Witch and the Wardrobe, the first book in C. S. Lewis' series *The Chronicles of Narnia.* After a couple of weeks I noticed that one student began to arrive late enough every day to miss the sitting but not the reading. One day I overheard him tell a classmate that while he didn't like the quiet sittings he loved the readings. At the end of that day I told the children that from now on we would begin with the reading and close with our quiet sitting. The next day the boy arrived right on time, a pattern that continued throughout his years at Sant Bani School.

In the British Infant System teaching students how to read relied on the whole-word/sight method. If you exposed students to a variety of printed material that had simple words repeated over and over, reading to them along the way, they would learn to distinguish what shapes formed which words and begin to read on their own. I provided graded readers to the two youngest students and happily spent time reading to them. After a few weeks, however, it became clear to me that I did not have the tools to assess their progress, if any. At the same time I understood that I had no idea what should distinguish, for example, a second grader from a third grader in math proficiency. While the students enjoyed working at the various stations for science, art, history, etc., how could I be certain they were truly challenging themselves to stretch and learn? What if the seventh grader was content to do fifth grade level problems all year—and I was responsible for his "academic growth?"

As the validity of Mildred's concerns became apparent I realized I needed help. Rather than reach out to Mildred for guidance I turned instead to my mom, who had been teaching second and third grades for decades, and was widely regarded as an excellent educator. As she was very supportive of the start-up of Sant Bani School, she eagerly lent her expertise, directing me to top-notch programs in math, science and language arts. She pointed out that training was available from publishing companies and that the fabled "teacher's editions" held many keys to goals, outcomes, strategies, levels, etc.

I followed through with my mom's advice, and soon I was teaching different students with various teacher's editions open in my lap. The two first graders and I would head upstairs to our bedroom where I successfully taught them how to read using the more phonetic-based approach of the Open Court method.[30] With the teacher's "bible" open on my knees, I would instruct Ben and Beverly while staying tuned to the activity of the four students in the room below. Now and then I had to stamp on the floor and pass down a gentle reminder to "stay on task." While this juggling of approaches began to yield positive results (and did have its charms), I continued to shy away from taking advantage of Mildred as a resource. My attitude would soon undergo a dramatic shift based on an experience that unfolded at Master Kirpal's school in India.

Winter Interlude: Six Weeks in India

In early February of 1974, Master Kirpal Singh hosted a worldwide conference on the Unity of Man in New Delhi, India. He had been president of the World Fellowship of Religions for many years, but now He felt it was time to create a major event *"with the noble purpose of fostering universal brotherhood leading to universal harmony."* He invited everyone to come who could, so we closed the school for six weeks in January/February while Karen and Chris and I flew to India to be a part of the historic and inspiring gathering of tens of thousands of people from all over the planet. When the conference was over and most everyone had gone home, several of us stayed on to visit *Manav Kendra*, Master Kirpal Singh's model community that, as noted at the beginning of this chapter, was located in the foothills of the Himalayan Mountains just outside Dehra Dun, India.

Karen, Chris, and I stayed on the premises of *Manav Kendra*, housed in empty rooms in the newly constructed Home for the Elderly. We had several opportunities to visit *Manav Vidya Mandir* to watch the school in action, to talk with staff and students, and to

---

[30] The Open Court Publishing Company based its approach on the Orton-Gillingham system that my mother was certified to teach. This method is described as "an intensive, sequential phonics-based system [that] teaches the basics of word formation before whole meanings."
(https://en.wikipedia.org/wiki/Orton-Gillingham).

attend a ceremony presided over by Master Kirpal Singh.[31] In particular I was fortunate to spend time with Miss Bhojwani Sati, the eminently practical yet extraordinarily wise sixty-year-old principal. She was very happy to carve out as much time as she could to talk with me about education at *Manav Vidya Mandir*.

Chris Bicknell receiving an orange from Master Kirpal Singh
Miss Sati stands between them

Early on in one of our many conversations I caught myself doing something that, unfortunately, had become a habit for quite some time. When Miss Sati brought up a specific area to discuss I felt a need to add some comment that would assure her I was already familiar with the subject. Through practice in high school and college I had become adept at saying something to indicate how bright and well-informed I was, whether I knew much about the subject or not. This time, however, I caught myself. As my mind shaped words that would have added nothing to the conversation except to shore up my *bona fides*, I recognized the pattern and silently said, "Stop!" I smiled internally and repeated, "Stop. Look. And Listen!"

The effect was amazing. Instead of half-listening while planning my response I suddenly heard <u>all</u> of what Miss Sati was sharing with me. As I wrote in my journal upon returning to New Delhi

---

[31] It was at this ceremony that Master Kirpal passed out oranges to all the students and faculty, and Chris was front-and-center ready to receive one too!

from Dehra Dun: "*2/13/74 – I am so anxious to please – to be in good favor – to say the right thing, etc. Now I feel ready to listen to what someone like Miss Sati has to say, rather than trying to impress with my own 'good' knowledge. Maybe this trip I can come more into my own and stand on my feet as an individual. That is, not always be walking on eggshells as regards what other people might be thinking of me. Need to lose the insecurity (humility helps here).*" Understanding how much there was to learn from Miss Sati, I recalled Mildred and all she might have to offer Sant Bani School. At once I was excited to build a working relationship with Mildred when we returned to the States.

In one of my first conversations with Miss Sati, I asked if all of the teachers at *Manav Vidya Mandir* were Satsangis. She replied, "Early on I asked Master Kirpal if I should hire only Satsangi teachers and he told me that I should put an advertisement in the newspapers and hire the most qualified candidates who applied. With a twinkle in his eye he added, 'Who knows, some of them might become Satsangis.' And two of them have become initiates."

After observing the rows of children in their uniforms working on their lessons or singing devotional songs[32] I had more questions for Miss Sati. I asked about the uniforms (standard for schools in India) and she explained that these children were from families that were so poor that the school outfits were by far the best clothes they had. Although issued by the school and therefore school property, the children were allowed to keep them.

I wondered if she ever had discipline problems and she responded that as they are children they do quarrel sometimes, and she helped students understand that the person doing the teasing was losing more than the recipient. She shared that she had asked one student to leave, which was very hard. He had been verbally abusing others, calling them names, using foul language, etc. He had been asked to stop many times but could not seem to help himself. Ultimately she and the staff concluded that he was "polluting the school atmosphere," which not only impacted him negatively but affected others adversely as well. As it was not healthy for the

---

[32] Scenes of this visit, including the children singing, are available at: https://santbaniashram.org/videos-of-the-master/. Scroll down to the film titled "Master Kirpal Outside His House Feb/March 1974" and advance the film to 17:25 to experience the children singing at *Manav Vidya Mandir*.

boy to continue his behavior or for others to be subjected to it, *Manav Vidya Mandir* dismissed him.

I asked her if the program had adopted any innovative practices and she replied with enthusiasm that it had. When the children studied geography she did not follow the textbooks alone but preferred a cross-disciplinary approach. For example, if they were studying the lives of saints like Mira Bai[33] or Guru Nanak,[34] the children located where the saints were born on the map, where they traveled, what the surrounding countryside looked like and what the social conditions were wherever they went.

Next she showed me a classroom where students, sitting on the floor, were working in pairs to practice their multiplication tables while the teacher circulated around the room to gently guide or respond to questions. She was very excited about this as it was truly breaking from the norm: a teacher in front of rows of 40+ desks drilling the students over and over again. As this hardly seemed innovative for schools in the U.S. I wondered how the Indian system of education worked and asked Miss Sati to please explain it.

Since the government sets the curriculum, the Education Department of the State of Uttar Pradesh presented *Manav Vidya Mandir* a fixed program to deliver at all levels and periodically examined the children using standardized tests. At that time both elementary and secondary education in India was geared toward national exams taken by students at various times after 10th grade. For the vast majority of students, their numerical score on that exam determined their future in terms of higher education and/or civil service employment. Mostly the exams tested a student's ability to memorize a broad array of facts and write those out in a timed exam. I now understood a phenomenon that previously had been puzzling: while in New Delhi I had seen many adolescents (in courtyards and on flat rooftops) reading aloud from a book, pacing to and fro, for hours on end. They were memorizing long passages of, for example, Shakespeare, so that they could write out verbatim entire sections for the national exam. In this context the student pairs were more revolutionary than at first glance: the students in *Manav Vidya Mandir* were being empowered to collaborate rather

---

[33] Mira Bai (1498-1546) was a famous sixteenth century woman saint of India.
[34] Guru Nanak (1469-1539) was the first of the ten Sikh Gurus.

than be drilled by the teacher. This was right in line with the school's published *Prospectus and School Rules*, which, understanding that children are "the future builders" of the nation provided an atmosphere where students developed "a sense of fellow-feeling and service of humanity."[35]

In addition to the subjects outlined by the government the program included art, sewing, agriculture and physical education. Curious about the latter I asked Miss Sati what the students were taught. She explained that the P.E. program expressed a healthy attitude toward competition with the goal being for each child to do her or his best. Recently the school had held some "junior Olympics" where the emphasis was on personal achievement rather than "the pride of victory or despair over defeat." The grand finale was a game of musical chairs involving all the staff including Miss Sati. She smiled as she added, "One can imagine how the children enjoyed seeing their teachers and principal running around the chairs, scrambling for a place to sit each time the music stopped!"[36]

As the time to visit and learn at *Manav Vidya Mandir* came to a close Miss Sati showed me a beautiful hand-made card that the children and staff presented to Master Kirpal for his birthday. She explained that he returned the card with an unexpected donation from his own pocket, after writing on the bottom of the card, *"Be Good. Do Good. Be One."* As Miss Sati, another teacher and I looked at the inscription Miss Sati suddenly said, "You know this applies to us also, not just the children." I took her observation as a wonderful recap of all that I had learned in my six weeks in India and was eager to get back to New Hampshire and plunge into the classroom once again. At the same time I was more than ready to begin consulting with Mildred in earnest, and that is exactly what happened.

---

[35] From the printed *Prospectus and School Rules of Manav Vidya Mandir*.

[36] Conversation with Miss Sati in February, 1974. I came to understand that events like staff musical chairs function as powerful pedagogy for participants and observers alike. It is important for children to have teachers who can have fun and not be afraid to poke fun at themselves. I am reminded of the long-standing "tradition" at SBS where faculty and staff perform an original skit for students on Halloween the content of which is almost always a gentle satire of a school event such as Projects Period or the All School Mountain Climb. The sillier the adults are the more the students enjoy the performance.

The Second Half of Year One

Everyone—students, parents and I—was very happy to be back in school after the long mid-winter holiday. One of the first things I did was check in with Mildred to go over what I was teaching at which level, and how. She agreed 100% with the counsel my mother had given and was delighted with the curricular materials I was using for the different grades. With the teacher's guides as reference points I could see that all the students were making measurable progress as I considered current work against benchmarks from earlier in the year.

In the spring we welcomed a visitor for two weeks: John Walker, a young Satsangi from California who had been in India with Karen, Chris and me and who was very interested in teaching as a career. He stayed as a guest at the ashram and spent time with us every day. John brought fresh ideas including something that was to become a staple of the SBS experience: drama. Under John's guidance students wrote and performed short skits that we all enjoyed. John brought more art into the day, including tactile experiences like shaping the mud that was so readily available into intriguing sculptures.

John Walker directing Eric and Chris to be tall trees

During John's visit we talked about the classroom, what was going well and what should be improved. We understood how critical it was to have an individualized approach given that the six students were each in such different places academically and socially. Perhaps the most powerful piece of pedagogy was how, given a supportive environment that encouraged taking risks, the students were learning from each other.

Recalling the P.E. program at *Manav Vidya Mandir* I reached out to my *alma mater*, New Hampton School, to enquire if we could use their gym. They responded that they would be happy to host us as long as there was no conflict with their own need for the facility. As Friday mornings were best for both schools, every week the six students, Chris (now 4) and I would pile into our yellow Saab 99 and take the back roads over to New Hampton. Some students were quite accomplished in various athletic activities as sports were already part of their routine. Others just needed the opportunity to dive in, and so they did. For an hour and a half we would shoot baskets, throw Frisbees, play catch, have contests to see who could throw a tennis ball furthest or with the most accuracy (or both!), run races, do calisthenics, play freeze tag, keep-away, dodge ball, Red Rover, Red Light/Green Light, and it seemed as if the children could never get enough.

One of the wonderful things of starting before the Stone Building was ready was that it allowed us to help with the construction as well as watch the structure grow. More than one recess was spent loading stones from a distant rock pile onto a rickety trailer pulled by an old red tractor. The students would jump on the trailer and back we would go to unload. This was a "hands-on" (at times even finger-pinching!) example of experiential learning at its best.

As we approached the end of the first year a number of routines had fallen into place, including calling adults by their first name and removing "outside" shoes at the door. These characteristic SBS traits were not a result of carefully thought-out pedagogy but came about by chance or necessity.

A few months before SBS opened Karen, Chris and I visited friends in Rockport, Massachusetts. At that time their 3-year-old daughter was going through a phase where she called her parents by their first names. Chris was intrigued and so began to call us "Karen" and "Kent." We assumed he would grow out of it if we ignored it, so we did. He continued using our first names, however, and we grew accustomed to it. When school began Chris, though only 3-and-a-half, was in the school room (his home) daily. As he called me "Kent" it seemed natural to have the students do so as well, and it has been what SBS has done ever since.[37]

Like the school buildings today, the first "classroom" sat on a hill surrounded by dirt paths. With any kind of precipitation all the dirt, sand, mud and slush was tracked into the building. Given that our house was doubling as school during the day and home in the evening, we requested that students and adults remove their outside shoes as soon as they entered. This also became a staple of SBS behavior. To visitors who wondered if there were a religious aspect to this we would say that it was simply an effort to leave the mud and dirt outside![38]

In May Mildred and my mom suggested I formally assess progress through some kind of standardized test so I ordered Stanford Achievement Tests for each grade. When one family strongly objected to any kind of testing based on their own experiences in public school I explained that these were tools to evaluate the effectiveness of my teaching rather than to put any kind of label on their child. I was happy to see that all the students were able to handle the material on the tests with ease.

As the year rushed to a close it was clear that everyone was excited about the success of the program and eager to occupy the Stone Building in September. After watching the walls go up, stone-by-stone, the roof go on and the windows and doors go in, we were anxious to move in ourselves. The students were happy to hear that more students wanted to enroll for the coming year as it appeared that the school was meeting a local need. Beverly, our one girl, was thrilled to hear that the gender balance would improve in year two. We wondered if this was, perhaps, in answer to a lunchtime prayer she offered in the middle of the year: "Dear God, I love this school—but would you please send more girls!"

---

[37] In the first couple of decades a few parents wondered if students would have more respect for teachers if they were addressed using surnames. We responded that respect comes from the quality of the relationship, and that having students and faculty on a first-name basis creates an atmosphere that is more conducive to learning and respecting each other. Less frequently a parent would suggest that we should adopt a school uniform as this would be "good" for the students. That suggestion disappeared at the turn of the century.

[38] On the other hand, guests entering the Satsang Hall (the main building of the ashram) are expected to remove their shoes as a sign of respect.

At the end of the last day of the first year Karen, Chris and I said good-bye to the six students (some of whom we would see frequently over the summer) and closed the front door with the realization that it had really happened: Sant Bani School was up and running!

Looking back over the year I reflected on how much I had learned from Miss Sati during my time in India and how I was so eager to connect with Mildred. Much like my mom, Mildred became a tremendous resource rather than a threat as we communicated at length over the summer, and I was thrilled when she decided to teach full-time at Sant Bani in the fall.[39]

An Outside Perspective

**Sant Bani Ashram Reaches Out
Into the Field of Education**
by David Graves
The Trumpeter, November 29, 1973

"The most important thing about education is its relation to life... A child is the center of creative life and needs to be opened as a flower is opened, gently, by sympathy, not by force."

These words, spoken by the Indian holy man Sant Kirpal Singh, first took seed June 21, 1972, at the inauguration of his first school in India. Since then, however, these thoughts have taken root in America at Franklin's Sant Bani Ashram, one of the Master's two religious communities in this country.

Ashram initiates refer to Kirpal Singh as "Master." One of his initiates since 1968 is Kent Bicknell, principal and only teacher of the ashram's new school which opened its doors on Sept. 10. Kent's living room is the school's only classroom.

"The school should be a home of teachers and students who reflect in their studies, and on the playground and in their daily lives, the cherished virtue of humility," spoke the Master again, inaugurating his school in India.

---

[39] Though very different personalities, Mildred and my mom got along so well that during her first year teaching at SBS Mildred lived with my parents in New Hampton. Subsequently Mildred stayed at the ashram during the week and returned to her home in Canterbury for weekends.

Kent is vegetarian. So is his wife, Karen, his son, Chris, and their pet hamster and Husky dog, along with the six children Kent teaches, only one of whom does not have initiate parents.

Before assuming his new work at the ashram, Kent was N.H. Day Care Consultant for two years.[40] "On the whole, the children I teach here are very gentle. I saw a lot of rage from the children I worked with in Concord," he said, reaching out to give a snippet of vegetable to his hamster.

The sign outside the entrance to the ashram reads, "WELCOME TO SANT BANI ASHRAM. Please don't kill our neighbors, the birds, fish, and animals." A gentle reminder of the Master's teachings on "the cherished virtue of humility" or doing unto others what you would have them do unto you.

The first lesson of the day at the school begins on "a spiritual basis," usually a reading by Kent from the life of a saint, whether it be Christian, Buddhist or Hindu. "The way a child plays reflects whatever he or she is exposed to at home, whether it's TV's *Rat Patrol* or a reading from a holy book," Kent commented. "The teacher's responsibility is to provide opportunities for the child's growth," he added.

After the reading, there's five minutes of silence, "an opportunity to think about God," as Kent described the experience. By late morning, the children are immersed in language arts or mathematics, each rotating on a daily lesson plan explicitly designed for his or her level of attainment. The six children under Kent's care range in grades from first through seventh.

Kent relies heavily on "Unifix" mathematical games to reinforce practical learning skills. A child might learn about mathematical units such as tens, twenties, etc., by manipulating different colored blocks according to numbers thrown on dice. The principle behind the game stresses abstract reasoning in the place of counting "apples and oranges" together, so often confusing to a youngster's mind.

Kent tries to work with each child individually, quite often unexpectedly involving the group as a whole. "It's eye-opening to watch the fascination with which the older students view the learning process going on between the younger students and myself," Kent said. Quite often an older student will pitch in to help a younger one understand Kent's point.

---

[40] Prior to SBS I worked at Merrimack Valley Day Care Center in Concord for two years, followed by one year as a Child Care Consultant for the State of New Hampshire.

After the morning's individual instruction is done, Kent reads another story to the group as a whole, ending with a discussion of the various possible meanings of the story. The current reading is from C. S. Lewis' *The Chronicles of Narnia*, a group of fairy tales about child princes and princesses, talking animals and their struggle to overcome evil with the help of a divine spirit.

The afternoon's work is much the same as the morning's, but each child exercises a greater free choice of activity. "I keep giving the children free choices until finally they choose what I want," Kent explained with a smile.

Before he came to the ashram, Kent graduated from Yale University. Last year he completed his MA studies in early childhood education at Goddard. During his work with the state in Concord, Kent discovered "how much children like me and how much I like them." He was a natural for starting the ashram school.

The school has been accredited by the New Hampshire Department of Education this fall and is open to all. "Nominal fees should be charged from the children who can afford to pay," the Master has stated, but financial hardship is no barrier to admittance.

"The best education is that which teaches us that the end of knowledge is service... another name for love and fellowship, which constitute the very essence of personal and social life," — again the Master's words, now in practice at the ashram school.

At present work is progressing in building a schoolhouse behind the school's temporary quarters in the Bicknell house. At the foundation of that building lie the gentler, more compassionate virtues of life—"sympathy," "humility," and "service," fertile soil for the natural growth of virtuous human beings under the inspiration of the Master, Sant Kirpal Singh.[41]

---

[41] This is the full article as it appeared in *THE TRUMPETER, Franklin-Tilton-Northfield, N.H.* at the end of the school's third month in operation. Accompanying the article was a black and white photograph of the Stone Building under construction.

Chapter II: The Second Year (1974-75)

Master Kirpal Singh (1894-1974)

On the 21st of August we received news that Master Kirpal Singh, founder of both the ashram and the school, had passed away in India. While Satsangis operate from a world view that understands the soul as immortal, this was very challenging for everyone as Master Kirpal had been so helpful in so many areas. At that time, and for the next couple of years, the Satsangis connected with Sant Bani Ashram were not aware of anyone who could properly convey the outer and inner teachings of Sant Mat. The story of the emergence of Sant Ajaib Singh as Master Kirpal's successor in 1976 and the subsequent role he played in both SBS and the ashram has been well documented in a number of places.[42] For those involved in the school and the ashram the reality in late August was that we had clear guidance for both organizations to move forward.

Summer Preparations

Over the summer I enrolled in an intensive workshop in Tarrytown, New York, hosted by Open Court Publishing Company. While Ben and Beverly had learned to read during the first year I was eager to go beyond instructing from a teacher's guide open in my lap and hoped to acquire tools needed for a more comprehensive approach. I learned a great deal from the instructors and gained a lot of confidence in the Open Court method which, as noted earlier, is a phonetics-based program.[43] I was drilled in the fact that the 26 letters of our alphabet can combine in 90 different ways to form the 43 basic sounds of English. I learned how to engage students in fast-paced games (using Open Court props) where they would learn all the variant spellings to make the sounds, and then how to combine them into whole words. The instructors explained that the founder of Open Court was disappointed at how

---

[42] See, e.g., Russell Perkins, *Impact of a Saint* (1980), Kent Bicknell, *Rainbow On My Heart* (2002).
[43] See Chapter I.

backward American schools seemed compared to what his young children had been learning in the schools they attended in Europe. Finding *Dick and Jane* primers uninspiring ("Run, Spot, run!") he sought an approach that would allow children access to better literary content at a younger age, and so chose the phonetic approach as a way to help children "unlock" the science of reading more effectively.

I was an enthusiastic student as I now had a better understanding of how much I needed to learn. An intriguing aspect of the workshop was that there was very little room for discussion. Participants were there to be drilled in the Open Court approach and the only questions tolerated were around putting the method into practice.[44] By the afternoon of the first day I stopped asking questions and absorbed as much information as I could of a program that was effective in teaching most students how to read, provided students with excellent skills for writing such as proofreading, starting prompts, etc., and that had high quality literary content throughout.

The workshop stressed ten points as keys for the success of the "Open Court Philosophy." These included: using an integrated multi-sensory approach; blending whole class time with small group and individual work; utilizing "hot" teaching (based on accelerated timing, lots of movement and continual circulation

---

[44] While I was accustomed to teachers who encouraged questions as a foundation for learning, this was a different pedagogy. The object of the workshop was to transmit the Open Court method and the instructors were "teaching to the middle." To be successful they needed to be sure that the majority of the participants (almost all were classroom teachers) left knowing how to apply the Open Court model. There was no time for seemingly extraneous questions or to coax along those who had trouble grasping the concepts. This was my first experience with something that was cited often in my doctoral program at Boston University: educational publishing companies are the driving force behind what students in American schools learn. The companies are intensely competitive, so it is important that teachers are well-trained in their system. If it is a good program, standardized tests scores in school districts go up and more and more schools want to adopt an approach that helps students achieve higher scores in math, language arts, science and social studies.

among the children); reading high quality literature; and keeping administration and parents informed and involved.[45]

As the workshop progressed and more context was provided for the ten keys I found that they amplified my nascent educational philosophy. The instructors taught us to "*Continually use positive reinforcement through a self-correcting approach. Don't say anything to a child about a mistake until after you have said something positive. Every day each child must have successful experiences. At the same time, every day each child needs an opportunity to reflect on what was correct and to figure out for himself how to correct things that need correction.*"[46] We learned how to teach via "*a multi-sensory approach where lessons are reinforced through seeing/hearing/saying/doing*" at the same time we embraced "*a correlated language arts system that includes reading, writing, listening, speaking and composition. This last, composition, includes spelling, punctuation, grammar, usage and sentence structure.*"[47]

We were taught that it was critically important to have an open mind about each child's potential: "*Make no assumptions about what your children do and do not know. Keep an open mind and just start teaching. 'Initial Presentation' and 'Direct Teaching'*[48] *help you do this. Begin the year with a review. Teach quickly, observing and evaluating each child at all times. Keep teaching, and do not get into what this child needs or doesn't need at your 'Initial Presentation' stage. It does not matter what system a child is coming into your school from, etc. Too often we make a judgement early in the year about a child and that sticks throughout; i.e. we lower our expectations. You need to constantly remind yourself to have open expectations for each child. Don't start putting each child into watertight compartments like, 'slow... average... fast,' etc.*"[49]

As the workshop came to a close I took stock of how much information had been shared for teaching language arts at all levels of elementary school. Though somewhat overwhelmed I was thrilled to have so many new techniques at my fingertips. I recalled how several friends had encouraged me to learn a craft or go to

---

[45] From the spiral-bound notebook I kept during a training session presented by the Open Court Publishing Company in Tarrytown, New York, at the end of July/beginning of August, 1974.

[46] *Ibid.*

[47] *Ibid.*

[48] By this point we all had been drilled in the Open Court techniques known as "Initial Presentation" and "Direct Teaching."

[49] July/August Notebook.

trade school rather than go back to college[50] and I realized I was learning a trade: the time-honored role of "educator."

On the long drive home I compared the British Infant System workshop I had taken the summer before and the session just completed. Both shared a fundamental commitment to educating the whole child while recognizing the individuality of each. While the British Infant System relied heavily on a child's innate curiosity to motivate learning, the Open Court approach gave the teacher many ways to convey essential skills that engaged students completely while they learned, as well as benchmarks for assessing growth along the way. I appreciated the value of blending models to build a personal approach that worked for both the teacher and the students. I reflected on how Miss Sati in India and Mildred Meeh in New Hampshire had done just that, and how eager I was to learn from them. I could hardly wait for school to begin!

Over the summer we added seven new students to the original six. These were Mira and Todd in 1st, Richard (with Bev and Ben) in 2nd, Julie (with Thomas) in 3rd, Stephanie (with Joey) in 4th, and Andrea and Scott in 7th. With Peter moving to 6th and Eric to 8th, we now had students in every grade except 5th. As August rushed to a close we madly put the finishing touches on the Stone Building and Sant Bani started to feel like a "real school."

Equally exciting was that our staff numbers would be doubling with the addition of Mildred as the second full-time teacher. Since returning from India in February, I had been in frequent communication with Mildred and was thrilled that she would be bringing her extraordinary combination of teaching excellence, graceful presence, creativity and humor to SBS on a daily basis. Without doubt Mildred delivered everything I could hope for and more. Her impact on SBS continues today.

What Mildred DeVos Meeh Brought to Sant Bani School

In the early 1900s Mildred's family emigrated from France in search of a new life. Her father, Auguste DeVos, a Protestant minister who worked for the Salvation Army for some time, hoped to

---

[50] See Introduction.

find a society less under the influence of both alcohol and the prevailing Catholic religion. Auguste came to America first, and then sent for his wife, Marceline, and their three sons. They settled in Rhode Island where Auguste earned a living preaching in French to Canadian mill workers as he traveled by horse and buggy throughout southern New England. Mildred was born in Woonsocket on November 5, 1913.[51]

Mildred enrolled in Temple University in Philadelphia where she met William Meeh, a night school student drawn, like Mildred, to the teachings of the Quakers. They fell in love and on March 30, 1942, Reverend Auguste DeVos presided over their marriage in Fall River, Massachusetts. Before either could finish college Bill was drafted to fight in World War II. Taking advantage of newly enacted Congressional legislation, Bill registered as a Conscientious Objector (C.O.) rather than enter the military. Initially the Civilian Public Service Program assigned him to work in a fire tower in Campton, New Hampshire. Living conditions in the primitive cabin were challenging for a young married couple, so Bill happily accepted an opportunity to work with patients at Brattleboro Retreat in Vermont. With other C.O.s, Bill and Mildred rented a house and began to build a small community of like-minded people. They became involved in the "Victory Gardens" of the day and then gardening in general. When the war ended the Meehs decided to continue working with the land on a larger scale as dairy farmers.

In 1950 Bill and Mildred acquired a large parcel of land that had once belonged to the Shaker Community in Canterbury, New Hampshire. In partnership with a fellow C.O. they started a dairy farm, but after a few years off many hardships and challenges, they decided it was time to find another livelihood. At a Quaker Meeting in Concord they met a family who was looking for a place for their two sons for the summer. The Meehs offered to host the boys and it worked out really well. Given how much they enjoyed this experience they decided to open a school, understanding it would take some time to prepare. They sold the cows in 1959 and went back to school at Keene State College, temporarily relocating to Marlboro, New Hampshire, to be closer to the campus.

---

[51] I am grateful that Tim Meeh was willing to share details about his mother's life prior to coming to Sant Bani. The majority of this section is based on information conveyed during conversations with him.

While earning her B.Sc. in Education Mildred worked for a year at High Mowing School in Wilton, New Hampshire, the oldest Waldorf boarding school in the country.[52] The Waldorf system of education was developed in Germany in the early 1900s by Rudolph Steiner. The emphasis was on nurturing the whole child through a curriculum geared to the developmental level of each student. The following excerpts from the current Mission and Vision Statements of High Mowing School capture many of the essential components of a Waldorf education:

> We utilize an approach to learning that is based on an understanding of the developing human being and the changing world around us. We offer an experiential and vigorous program of arts-infused academics within a small and friendly school community, where young people and adults have the opportunity to form authentic and meaningful relationships. We provide a complete program of humanities, math, science, world languages, fine, practical and performing arts, diverse movement education and individual interest electives — all immersed in and surrounded by nature.
>
> We recognize and nurture the highest potential in each person. We are a community where students discover who they are and develop the capacity for living fully into the future as it unfolds for them.[53]

It is clear that certain elements of the Waldorf pedagogy resonated with Mildred. The combination of a degree in education and a year working at High Mowing provided a perfect blend for what was to become Mildred's hallmark: strong academics infused with a passion for the arts, drama and music in a curriculum designed to nurture the potential of every child.

Now feeling more prepared, the Meehs returned to Canterbury and opened Horizon's Edge Country Home School in 1960.[54] The nascent school grew and a community of people who shared their

---

[52] Founded in 1942 High Mowing was the first boarding and secondary Waldorf school in the U.S. See founder Beulah H. Emmet's history of the school at https://cdn.media78.whipplehill.net/ftpimages/673/misc/misc_107155.pdf
[53] https://www.highmowing.org/page/about/mission-vision-values
[54] Horizon's Edge operated until 1990 even though Mildred left in 1974 to teach full-time at Sant Bani School.

world view developed around them. Friends from the Conscientious Objector group in Brattleboro stayed in touch through a newsletter, and some of them came to Canterbury. Bill and Mildred subdivided their land and sold to friends, and then hired C.O.s from the Vietnam War to help with building projects as the school expanded.

Horizon's Edge was very successful. Along with a strong foundation in academics there was an emphasis on art, music, dance, drama, experiential learning and immersion in nature. Creativity and collaboration were key components as students and faculty alike worked on projects. Throughout the program there was an emphasis on quality. While Mildred embraced the concept of process being as important as the product, she always held the final product to very high standards.[55] The success of Horizon's Edge took a personal toll; as Mildred explained it, the school became such a force in their lives that it overtook their marriage, and she and Bill divorced in 1971.

As noted in the introductory chapter, Russell and Judith Perkins were very happy to have found Horizon's Edge School as an alternative for their children, Miriam and Eric. Judith began to work at Horizon's Edge and helped Mildred with many aspects of the school. In turn, Mildred began to connect more and more with the spiritual teachings she found at Sant Bani Ashram and, after a time, made a life choice to become a Satsangi. Coupled with Mildred's strong background in educational theory and practice and her commitment to the spiritual teachings of Sant Bani Ashram it made perfect sense for Russell and Judith to ask her to be involved with Sant Bani School.

Anyone who knew Mildred was struck by her abundant *joie de vivre* accompanied by a wonderful sense of humor that seemed to be captured in her pronunciation of a favorite word: *bee-you'-tee-ful*. With an almost ever-present twinkle and smile she would share a humorous anecdote and burst out laughing again at the retelling. She delighted in the fact that while her family did not have a TV, her neighbors, the Shakers, did — and it was the elderly Shaker Sisters who signed up her three children to be members of the Mickey

---

[55] I recall attending a wonderful production of Shakespeare's *Midsummer Night's Dream* by a highly engaged (and very convincing) middle school student cast.

Mouse Club. Gleefully she talked about the time three of the Shaker Sisters, a sect known for modesty in dress, invited her to harvest cranberries and all three Sisters hiked their long skirts way up to wade out into the bog. She related that she learned to love both music and golf from her older brother Leon, and it was always fun to drive by Den Brae Golf Course and see Mildred out on the links, long silver braids flowing as she drove the ball.

Mildred Meeh

Mildred, who loved to travel and experience new things, had an adventurous spirit that embodied the concept of a "life-long learner." Late in life she made many trips to India and, on her own, to Morocco, Indonesia, England (where she studied for a summer in Cambridge) and, of course, to her beloved France. She loved being in community — the Quakers, Conscientious Objectors, Canterbury, Horizon's Edge, Sant Bani Ashram and Sant Bani School — but she also loved her solitude, her privacy. She understood that living requires balance and that often the most meaningful growth comes from the tension of competing forces. This meant she was comfortable encouraging each child to do her/his best at the same time she held each to very high standards. Students constantly worried about what grade she would give them at the same time that they really wanted to do their very best for Mildred. Time and again SBS graduates came back and talked about how grateful they were for the hard work they did in Mildred's courses and how much it helped build a foundation for what came after. Over and over again, she inspired almost everyone who came in contact with her.

In *The Story of Philosophy: The Lives and Opinions of the World's Greatest Philosophers*, writer Will Durant sums up Aristotle's thinking on excellence: *"Excellence is an art won by training and habituation: we do not act rightly because we have virtue or excellence, but we rather have these because we have acted rightly... we are what we repeatedly do. Excellence, then, is not an act but a habit."*[56] While I do not recall Mildred referencing this ancient wisdom there is no doubt that her pedagogy was built on the same principle.

Year Two

It was so exciting to open in a new space built for us (and by us) as we added new students and a brilliant seasoned teacher. The Stone Building consisted of a large room and, three steps down, an alcove, two tiny bathrooms, sinks and a small office. At the main entrance was a large stained-glass window of a beautiful swan, emerging from the water while reaching its wings up to the sun. A local Satsangi, Chris Grey, was learning the art of stained glass and made this for us. In the ancient tales of India the swan is cited as having a number of powerful qualities. While it lives on the earth it can soar into the heavens at will. It has great powers of discrimination and can use its beak to separate milk from water as well as find jewels hidden in the mud. The motivation behind making and giving the window to the school was loving kindness, and it is from this unsolicited gift, visible today in the main entrance of the renovated Upper Building, that SBS got its logo and its mascot. The window, with its play of light from either side, was a living testament to the power of a symbol, and coming in by the swan every morning was a great way to start each day.

After outside shoes were exchanged for slippers, coats were hung and lunches stored, we all sat together for the now "traditional" Morning Session. Readings over the year were from classics (or soon-to-be-so) like Lloyd Alexander's *Chronicles of Prydain*, C.S. Lewis' *Narnia* series, an adapted version of John Bunyan's 17th century classic, *The Pilgrim's Progress* (called *The Story of Little Christian*), *Tales of the Mystic East* (stories for children from the writings

---

[56] Will Durant, *The Story of Philosophy: The Lives and Opinions of the World's Greatest Philosophers* [1926], Simon & Schuster/Pocket Books (1991), p. 76.

of the spiritual teachers of Sant Mat), biographies of saints such as Guru Nanak and Swami Vivekananda, and *Great Swedish Fairy Tales*. One tale from this last, "The Seven Wishes" (about a foolish boy named Olle Niklasson whose wishes had unintended results), became such a favorite it was read annually for many years at the request of students.

When the reading was over we would have our time of quiet, and then talk about the day ahead. In the early days, Morning Session provided an opportunity to address community issues including incidents of hurt feelings, fair play, etc. along with a review of the day's schedule. Mildred explained that sitting in a circle was an ancient form of community building, as everyone faced everyone else and no one was staring at anyone's back. Sharing came naturally, and students and teachers were not afraid to say what was on their minds. It was easy to see that sitting on the same level and using first names for everyone were key ingredients in the creation of trust.

Kent playing the harmonium at Morning Session

After Morning Session we scattered for "classes" at several tables and chairs on the main floor and one table in the alcove. Given my recent training I taught language arts to grades 1-4 and Mildred taught the same for grades 6-8 (there was no 5th grader). Mildred taught the early grades math and I worked with the older students. We combined grades for history and science, with the latter being almost completely project-based.

43

Open Court in action

History was a specialty of Mildred's and she excelled at encouraging the students to create their own "textbooks" about whatever they were studying. After the class selected an ancient civilization Mildred would read source material to them while the students took notes. The next step would be to research it on their own to be able to write and draw about it. After completing multiple drafts (with draft illustrations) their work was captured in a final book that was often stunning. As noted, Mildred was a stickler for process and product: she expected each child to do her or his best to create a finished product of lasting beauty. Though students may have struggled with what could seem like endless drafts during the process, when they finished their book and watched others admire the quality and depth of their text and illustrations, their faces shone with pride.

Mildred introduced a number of important ingredients to the SBS blend including having specific blocks for art a couple of days a week. These "art blocks" were during the last period of the day and provided a variety of choices for something to do for a six- to eight-week period. Initial offerings included block printing and stained glass, and with the help of Karen Bicknell, weaving and sewing.

Block printing involved drawing a design that would transfer well to the medium. The design was copied onto a linoleum block and then carved out with a sharp tool. When ready, the block was inked so that prints on paper or cloth could be made. Many students became quite skilled at producing lovely prints and eventually the school created an annual SBS Block Print Calendar that was a big hit until the era of paper calendars faded. Students did well with artwork entered into local and state competitions, and even won a national award from a school supply company, which netted the school a plaque and a good deal more block printing material.[57]

Although creating stained glass pieces did not involve the use of lead and solder, children did learn to cut glass pieces to size. The first step was to draw a colorful "cartoon" of what they wished to create. Based on their design they chose colored glass, cutting to fit as needed, to recreate their cartoon by gluing small pieces onto an 8.5" by 12" piece of clear glass. Spaces between the colored pieces were filled in with black window putty to give the illusion of lead. As I learned the requisite skills from Mildred I was soon able to lead groups of students on my own.

The children created many exceptional works of art, some of which still grace the halls of SBS and the walls of alumni homes. Perched in the highest window of the Multi-Purpose Room in the Upper Building is a stained-glass window created for SBS by one of its earliest graduates (and one of the "original six"), Eric Perkins '79. The glass features a large stag in front of which a hunter, having laid down his crossbow, kneels. Eric copied this motif, based on a Scandinavian folktale of compassion toward all, from the design on the large Jøtul woodstove that provided heat for the Stone Building for years. The arts of block printing, stained glass, weaving and sewing continue today as an essential part of the SBS curriculum through choices offered during art classes and after-school enrichment blocks.

Music was another strength Mildred brought. While I sang and played guitar, dulcimer and harmonica, I had never learned to read music. Mildred introduced the recorder, and through that simple instrument taught every student to read and play music. I learned along with them so that I was able to teach a class the next year. While "homework" involving the recorder may have driven more than one family to distraction in those initial stages of shrill squeaks, the class soon learned to play sweet melodies that could

---

[57] Two students created a dual color piece that won a national award from the art supply company Dick Blick (www.dickblick.com).

be underwritten with the larger alto (and even tenor) recorders. For many students, learning the recorder became an entry point to taking lessons in another instrument as they could now read music. Students went on to excel in wind, brass, percussion and stringed instruments.

The first year I sang songs with the students, accompanied by either the guitar or dulcimer. Mostly we sang traditional folk tunes such as "Old Dan Tucker" and "Froggy Went a Courtin'." Mildred introduced harmony through the round. An early favorite, that still strikes home today, was "Make new friends, but keep the old. One is silver and the other is gold." When the thirteen students would break into three groups and sing that as a round the resulting harmony was audible proof of the power of many voices singing as one.

Drama and dance also became parts of the curriculum. In Mildred's year at High Mowing School she learned "Eurythmy," the specific performance art form taught at Waldorf Schools throughout the world.[58] After some discussion, we chose to introduce square dancing instead. I had learned all kinds of dance styles through my mother's free lessons for children in New Hampton and Mildred's hometown, Canterbury, was a hotbed for the resurgence of "contra dancing." With fifteen dancers (counting Mildred and me) we did not have quite enough for two "squares" of eight but we made do, dancing to records borrowed from my mother to songs that seem from another era:

> *Now all join hands and circle the ring.*
> *Stop where you are, give your honey a swing.*
> *Now swing that little gal behind you.*
> *Now swing your own,*
> *If you have found that she's not flown.*
> *Allemande left with the corner girl.*
> *Do-si-do your own.*
> *Now you all promenade with the sweet corner maid,*
> *Singing, "Oh, Johnny! Oh, Johnny! Oh!"*

As I recorded in a journal kept at the time, *"Monday, April 21st. Square dancing in the afternoon and it looked pretty good. I noticed that*

---

[58] See https://en.wikipedia.org/wiki/Eurythmy

_____ *was really into it; trying hard and enjoying it. I also noticed that people were really nice about changing partners, asking others politely, '_____, would you like to be my partner?'"*[59] Square dancing became more popular over the next couple of years as our population grew and high school grades were added.

Along with a seasoned strength in academics and music, art and drama, Mildred brought a zest for life that was infectious. When something was funny she whooped with a laugh that went through her whole body. Anyone who was at recess on a good day for sledding will probably never forget the picture of Mildred, her silver braids spilling out from a woolen cap, jumping on a sled at the top of our hill and laughing aloud all the way to the bottom. She did this with the same focus as a six-year-old and derived the same kind of full-body enjoyment from the experience.

Yet another Mildred "tradition" was established when she decided to read aloud during lunch. She began with the spell-binding (if harrowing) lengthy narrative, *South: The Endurance Expedition* by the British explorer Sir Ernest Shackleton. In an attempt to be the first men to traverse Antarctica in 1914, Shackleton and his crew spent almost two years facing every kind of peril the frozen pole could offer. After two months of lunchtime reading the crew, miraculously, made it through alive. If one is looking for "grit," those men had it in the extreme, and it was fun to see students re-enacting aspects of the journey in the snow during recess.

Early during the second year Mildred introduced what became a favorite game for rainy day recesses: *MURDER!* Participants sat in a circle facing each other, with one "murderer" amongst us. No one knew who it was other than the person who drew the designated card. The person who was "it" would wink at another player to kill them, trying to do so subtly enough so as not to be seen by anyone else in the circle. If you were winked at you had to die (usually dramatically!). The object was to be the last person standing. If a player thought s/he knew who was "it" s/he would say, "I have an accusation to make." If someone else were willing to "second" the accusation, then they both named the murderer aloud at the same moment. If they were wrong, both accusers died and the

---

[59] *SBS Journal for April-June 1975*, p. 20. This was a journal I kept for the latter portion of Year #2 at SBS.

game went on. If they were right, the game ended and a new hand was dealt. Initially we used playing cards with a jack signifying who was "it" but after a time I created a special pack of cards with hand-drawn figures that we used over and over again.[60]

It always intrigued me that Mildred, a Quaker committed to non-violence, enjoyed playing *MURDER* as much as the rest of us. While we never talked about this juxtaposition, over time I began to see it might be a question of balance. When Karen and I went to India for six weeks in 1974, our son Chris (age 4) had never been allowed to play with toy guns. One day during our stay at Sawan Ashram[61] in New Delhi, Chris came running into our room to proudly display a squirt gun that a boy living at the ashram had shared with him. Clearly there are limits to how much we can control, and perhaps we all need reminders not to take ourselves so seriously. Many years later I recall Craig Jaster (the dynamic Head of Performing Arts at SBS for 30 years) sharing with me how healthy it was for children to be able to do some things on stage that would not necessarily be appropriate in the hallways or classroom. Mildred was so well-balanced that she was always eager to experience the perspective of another person.

I was learning from Mildred and the students every day. Four-and-a-half-year-old Chris would visit often, and as he "worked" he had a tendency to sing softly to himself. One day I was teaching a group at a nearby table and I asked him to please be quiet. Mildred came to his defense and said how much she enjoyed hearing his sweet voice. It was one of the daily examples of the value of a different perspective.

In March Karen and I had our second child, Nicholas, who brought an abundance of joyful energy into our lives (and to the high school students who helped care for him when he was a toddler!). We were happy that the school now had a place of its own, as the four of us filled our small home. In the spring I began a doctoral program in curriculum development at Boston University. The courses were scheduled to be very user-friendly as they met

---

[60] As I look over the different illustrations on the cards in this pack today I wonder what educators in the 21st century would think of playing this game and using those cards with a group of students ages 7-13.

[61] Sawan Ashram was Master Kirpal Singh's headquarters in New Delhi. See Chapter I for more on our 1974 trip to India.

once a week in the evening for two hours. On Mondays I drove to Boston for a 4:30 class, stayed for a second at 6:30, and headed home at 8:30.

Almost all the courses were designed to allow us to apply what we were learning in our own setting. The professor in one class talked about how challenging it is to be aware of our own perspective and suggested we tape record a class to have a better sense of what was actually happening. I taped an Open Court class with two students in the alcove. When I played it back in the evening I was astonished at how many times I politely asked the students to pay attention in what, at times, was a wheedling voice. I decided to count the number of times I said "please" and stopped when I reached thirty in less than 15 minutes. What, I wondered, were the students learning from that kind of direction? Needless to say, I altered my approach, striving to be clear and direct. I paid more attention to Mildred and realized this is exactly how she had been teaching all along. Perspective. At the same time, as I noted in my journal, "*the over abundant energy of _____ springs from enthusiasm. It helps to remember that he really loves the work.*"[62]

As the year went on Mildred and I recognized that although we were teaching only 13 students, the spread across eight grades was such that we needed more help. Ann Matty joined us as a part-time teacher during the second half of the year, and Scott's mother, Gwen, came several days a week to help out. We covered more academic ground more effectively and were delighted with the results of the standardized testing administered toward the end of the year.

Both Mildred and I were so pleased with the progress students were making with the Open Court model that we wanted to share the approach with other educators. My mother helped us organize a one-day workshop and we were excited when several local public school teachers joined us for the day. They were intrigued by our "one room" school and eager to see what we had to share. The morning workshop was followed by a tasty vegetarian lunch (a new idea to some) and an afternoon session that was appreciated by all. It was our first experience of hosting a "Sant Bani Teacher Institute."

---

[62] *SBS Journal for April June 1975*, Tuesday, April 29, p. 29.

In late April the seven students in Grades 1-3 and I read the story "Androcles and the Lion." In this ancient tale (which has many incarnations) a runaway slave, Androcles, saves a lion and subsequently is spared by the lion when he must face it in Rome's famed *Circus Maximus*. The emperor is so impressed by their friendship that he frees them both. From my journal: *"We went through the 'Androcles and the Lion' dictation section where they had to write the longest and most difficult sentences to date. We did them all in 10 to 15 minutes. I was impressed with the speed and accuracy of the entire class. Then the group excelled at identifying subjects, verbs, and objects, and even sandwiched negatives. They handed in a good set of compositions of a gladiators' ring from the lion's point of view."*[63]

No doubt inspired by our reading of "Androcles," the first "formal" dramatic production at SBS, staged, rehearsed and performed in costume in front of a live audience was *St. Jerome and the Lion*. This is the delightful story of a Christian monk, St. Jerome, and his friendship with a lion. One day a lion came into the monastery and all the monks scattered except Jerome. The lion approached him and held up a front paw so that Jerome could see and remove a thorn. The two became companions, and Jerome gave the lion the task of guarding the monks' donkey during the day. One day the lion fell asleep and thieves stole the donkey. The monks accused the lion of eating the donkey, but, after a period of banishment from the monastery, the lion spotted the thieves with the donkey and alerted the monks so that all was well in the end. Mildred did a masterful job casting the story in different characters and for several of the students it was their first time memorizing lines, blocking out scenes, and getting and staying in character. The audience was most appreciative of the production and from then on drama too became a staple of an SBS education.

One day in early May we had two special visitors. In the morning, Arran Stephens, a Satsangi from Vancouver who had spent a lot of time with Master Kirpal Singh, came and shared interesting stories of his travels in India and what it was like to live at the ashram there. He also sang some *bhajans* (devotional songs) written by the Masters. In the afternoon Dudley Laufman of Canterbury came

---

[63] *SBS Journal for April-June 1975*, Tuesday, April 22, pp. 21-22.

and taught us traditional New England contra dances while sharing much local history.

Dudley Laufman at SBS

It was a full day, enjoyed by everyone. After school Mildred and I reflected on how important it was to keep a balance in our days, and that this day had seemed just right.[64]

Friday, May 9th
Began today with beautiful outside session. As kids arrived I gave them a choice of 1) going inside if they wanted to visit and chat; or 2) staying outside in silence and stillness, absorbing nature. Most chose to stay outside. It was a beautiful, bird-filled morning and the students enjoyed it (except for ___ , who ran around so much he had to go inside). Then we had a time of meditation outside. After we sat quietly I talked about being active at times and being passive at other times so that we can receive. We must learn to be still, as there are great forces that are silent.[65]

Wednesday, May 21st
Listened to the tape of the school presentation made by Arran Stephens about his time in India. It was so nice and simple and direct. Sometimes I feel we are afraid to be that way — we are conditioned to question. If we have got anything to say, let's put it right out front. Unity, unity, unity; love of All in all — how can we get it in school? How, so it carries over?
"Sant Bani School is dedicated to the CONCRETE REALIZATION of HUMAN UNITY."

---

[64] SBS Journal for April-June 1975, Thursday, May 8, pp. 37-38.
[65] SBS Journal for April-June 1975, Friday, May 9, p. 39.

How to achieve? How to come at it more from that point of view — in all areas — math, natural sciences, history, literature — unity in different modes?

St. Augustine said:

- In essentials UNITY.
- In non-essentials Liberty.
- In all things LOVE.[66]

Mildred teaching outdoors, with Ulf

As May rolled into June everyone's thoughts turned to the summer holiday. The question arose, however, as to where our one 8th grader, Eric, would go following his "graduation" from SBS. Throughout the year Russell, Judith, Mildred and I had been discussing the idea of starting a 9th grade the next year, adding a grade a year going forward. I consulted with some independent school colleagues and more than one advised us not to do it. It was not possible to run a high school by just extending the elementary staff. We were game however, and as the year closed we had a least two students prepared to enter: Eric and Carolyn, the older sister of our 7th grader, Andrea.

At the same time interest in the elementary program had grown to the point where we needed to expand. A two-story wood-framed building was designed to connect with the Stone Building, and a fieldstone fireplace was planned to help tie the two together aesthetically. Construction happened over the summer and when school opened in September we enrolled 31 students in grades 1-9 spread over a two-building complex that included several rooms.

[66] SBS Journal for April-June 1975, Wednesday, May 21, p. 53.

"I love you. But who are you?"

Toward the end of the year I found a small slip of paper on the floor with the above words written out in block letters. It was not signed, but something about it captured the spirit of SBS for me. I taped it to one of the free-standing wood columns in the Stone Building and there it stayed for many years. To me, like the swan window, it was a beacon that inspired daily.

An Outside Perspective

Sant Bani Construction
Sant Bani School Adds Space, Grade
by John W. Reid
Concord Monitor, Late Summer 1975[67]

SANBORNTON – The sounds of banging hammers and buzzing saws herald the approach of another school year at Sant Bani Ashram, nestled among the trees on a secluded hillside.

Two Sanbornton carpenters and several volunteers are building a two-story addition that will more than double the size of the present one-room school, providing two more classrooms and a library and reading center, said principal Kent Bicknell.

A large stone fireplace and chimney will be built up the back wall of the wood frame structure. Other expansions this summer include clearing a large athletic field from nearby woods.

Between 25 and 30 children have enrolled for the coming year. When the followers of the Sikh guru, Kirpal Singh, founded the school at the ashram in September, 1973, there were seven students.

"Every day begins with the spiritual reading and a period of quiet prayer or meditation," says a brochure explaining a school day. "Children are presented with the lives and teachings of the saints and scriptures of all races and religions." This year's class will be comprised of students from the Jewish, Catholic, Baptist and other Protestant faiths, said Bicknell.

"We talk a lot about the oneness of humanity," said Bicknell in a Monitor interview. "We all have God within us — that's the most important aspect, really."

---

[67] While the actual date is missing in the cropped article it is most likely mid-August.

53

The ashram's reverence for humanity extends to all life, not just man. One of the school's strongest rules concerns the lunch students bring each day — it must be strictly vegetarian. Even the Bicknell's dog, a Norwegian Elkhound named Ulf, lives — quite well by appearances — on grain, rice, cottage cheese and other vegetable leftovers.

The school, accredited by the N.H. Department of Education, stresses language arts and mathematics. Art, music — singing, playing the recorder and folk dancing — and handwork such as ceramics and weaving round out the curriculum.

Faculty members in addition to Bicknell include Mildred Meeh, who is responsible for bringing art and handcrafts to the school, Ann Matty and Robert Schongalla.

Why was the school started? "We felt we wanted to be sure children are getting a basic concept of reverence for all life," said Bicknell, his hair and bent wire-rimmed glasses sprinkled with sawdust. "We encourage a sense of service — helping others," explained Bicknell, adding that students learn "of people who made sacrifices in large or small ways — for the good of humanity."

The pupils who attended the school the first year it was in operation spanned Grades 1-7. This year the staff will begin a high school curriculum with two ninth-graders. The school is recruiting secondary grade students, but Bicknell warns, "Our high school is not everyone's cup of tea. If someone is looking for cheerleading, the social scene, the election of class officers and that type of thing, they're not going to find it here.

Instead, students will ponder specific and thorny issues like non-violence. "On the one hand, the Indian leader Mohandas Gandhi preaches non-violence. Yet Master Kirpal Singh says to be a soldier to help oppressed people is a noble thing," said Bicknell, citing an example. We will try to balance those ideas with tricky questions like Vietnam — where did that fit in?" he said.

Tuition at the school is $500 a year, but it costs $1,100 to provide each student's education for a year, he said. "Our local congregation helps cover the deficit, and if parents can pay more, they do," he said. "But people who can't don't feel pressured."

How successful is the school that preaches kindness and love to fellowman? "One thing I've noticed is that the children really feel secure. They know that no one is going to 'one up' them or dupe them," said mild-mannered Bicknell. "We get great comments like 'Oh, what a boring weekend I had,' and when the end of the school day comes they're really upset they had to stop what they're doing," he said.

Chapter III: The Third Year (1975-1976)

If the second year had felt more like a "real" school was happening, the third year solidified the building blocks of the SBS foundation. More than 30 students in grades 1-9 moving about in a setting that now included several rooms, two stories and a new playground was quite different than 13 students in a one-room school. As the challenges of scheduling French, Spanish, Algebra and U.S. History emerged so did the need for clearly defined class periods, lunch times and recesses, and the complexity of the daily schedule grew accordingly. Six-week holidays in the middle of the winter faded into the lore of Sant Bani!

Beyond the Satsangis who naturally gravitated to a school that supported their core values, other families began to hear about us and wanted their child(ren) to come. Seven children from Satsangi families were ready for first grade, and three from non-Satsangi families joined to create a starting class of ten. In addition, we now had two in 2nd, five in 3rd, three in 4th, two in 5th, two in 6th, two in 7th, three in 8th and two (soon to be three) in 9th.[68]

New Faculty

We strengthened our faculty with the addition of Robert Schongalla, who joined Mildred and me in late summer as a full-time teacher, and then Deborah Asbeck. Along with Robert and Debbie, Gerald Boyce and Russell Perkins joined the staff as part-time teachers.

Robert brought a life-long understanding of science and the environment that neither Mildred nor I could begin to match. He had been teaching French (and ceramics) at nearby New Hampton School and was delighted to jump right in and teach Earth Science

---

[68] Students for 1975-76 included Chris, Per, Paul, Faith, Leah, Becky, Matt D., Mike, Corey and Christina in 1st (with Kara to join later in the year); Mira and Todd in 2nd; Richard, Bev, Ben, Bethany and Jason in 3rd; Julie, Thomas and Michael in 4th; Stephanie and Geraldine in 5th; Heather and Elaina in 6th; Suzi and Peter in 7th; Andrea, Scott and Scott in 8th (with Lisa joining later in the year); and Eric, Carolyn and Gina (who came in October) in 9th.

to the 9th graders as well as language arts, social studies and ceramics. Robert, with his gentle manner and abundant kindness, was a perfect fit for the school and everyone loved what he brought. Class included field trips and work in the garden, and, as Eric Perkins recalled years later, the Earth Science class with Robert that year made such an impression on him that it "played a role in my ending up in a career in environmental science."[69]

Mildred and I offered training in the Open Court system for our new teachers and Robert was happy to take over 3rd grade Language Arts. As has been noted, Open Court was built on quality literature and the textbooks for all grades included high level excerpts from a variety of sources. This made it easy for both teachers and students to engage fully with the readings and reflect orally and in writing on how literature relates to life. Robert's class of five thrived on the experience.

Over the years Robert went on to become head of the Science Department and teach many subjects including French literature, middle school science, ceramics, gardening and bee keeping among others. He created lots of opportunities for field work in science that impacted students for decades. Robert led the way for SBS students to be among the first to contribute to the longitudinal "White Pine Study" at UNH (the Forest Watch Program[70]) so, over time, students really could feel that the work they were doing had an impact well beyond their small school at the end of the road.

Debbie Asbeck spent her formative years in Venezuela and then came north to attend Colby College in Waterville, Maine. A number of students from Colby became interested in Master Kirpal Singh, including Debbie, who moved near Sant Bani Ashram after she graduated. When the school needed extra help Debbie was happy to sign on as a part-time teacher. As the fall progressed Ann Matty went on maternity leave and Debbie took over 1st grade social studies, 3rd grade math and a combined 5th/6th language arts. With her strong background in Spanish she began to teach simple phrases to the 1st graders, creating story books with them. In com-

---

[69] Communication with the author, April 3, 2017.
[70] http://www.forestwatch.sr.unh.edu/pine/pinesci.shtml

bination with the high school course I introduced for two 9th graders, the SBS Spanish program that flourishes today was up and running.

Debbie continued to share her wit, wisdom and exceptional teaching skills with students and staff for decades. Whether teaching beginners, reading advanced literature or helping students drill for the SAT, Debbie's love for the Spanish language and culture was apparent, and she chaired the Department of World Languages. Many SBS graduates continued Spanish in college, or traveled in Central and South America as well as Spain. Along with Spanish (and French on occasion), Debbie shared her enthusiasm for creating nutritious goodies in countless Art Blocks and Clubs and at middle-school overnights at Camp Wilmot.

At some point Debbie decided to take reading a book at Morning Session to a new level. Every other year she would choose a novel such as *Mrs. Frisbee and the Rats of NIMH* or *I, Juan de Pareja* and proceed to map out a number of games and challenges based on the book. Then the fun would begin. With upperclassmen serving as captains, teams were created through drawing names to ensure that each team had at least one student from every grade.[71] Throughout the several weeks it took to read the book, teams battled for points in good-natured competition that covered everything from SBS lore to trivia to ways for each team's members to get to know each other. The grand culmination was an afternoon of lively Debbie-invented "field games" that connected with the book. Some iterations even had special T-shirts designed for the event. Then, without fail, an even grander culmination took place at a Morning Session when Debbie awarded prizes of goods she had baked herself, with something for each participant so that everyone partook of the delicious treats that captured Debbie's giving nature so well. Other titles Debbie read over the decades included *The View from Saturday, The Avion My Uncle Flew, Sticks, The Mostly True Adventures of Homer P. Figg, Escape from Mr. Lemoncello's Library, Chasing Vermeer, The True Blue Scouts of Sugar Man Swamp* and *Ghosts I Have Been.*

Someone once made a calling card for Gerald Boyce that described him as a carpenter and "a student of life." He was. Gerald

---

71 That is, they were vertical groupings rather than horizontal.

grew up in Franklin, New Hampshire, and, after graduating from high school, worked at a saw shop there for years. Along the way, he traveled west to live with Native Americans, learned the universal language of Esperanto, and was an avid reader of the Indian philosopher Jiddu Krishnamurti. Gerald became a vegetarian at a young age when a neighbor asked him to slaughter some chickens for her. He told me he couldn't do it, and, with a twinkle in his eye, added, "I decided right then that I would never eat meat again until I got hungry enough to kill the animal myself. And I haven't been that hungry yet!"

As noted in Chapter I, Gerald was the first person Karen and I met when we came to Sant Bani Ashram in 1968. Our initial impression was that we were seeing Gandalf come to life, or Walt Whitman reincarnated! He moved through this world with the grace of a dancer, and his was the Dance of Life. Gerald, it turned out, was an avid student of mathematics and a natural fit to teach high school students. Always thoughtful, perceptive and patient, he met each student at her or his own level and helped them progress through the program, starting with Algebra I for the 9th graders.

Russell joined us to teach U.S. History to the 8th and 9th grade students. As a representative of Master Kirpal Singh he had been counseling spiritual seekers very effectively for a number of years and knew how to engage young minds in discussions on a wide variety of topics. No one was better equipped to help students "ponder specific and thorny issues like non-violence" as taught by Gandhi, balanced with the complexities of our presence in Vietnam.[72] While Russell's impact on SBS will be discussed in more detail in the next chapter, with these additions to the faculty the school confidently moved forward.

The Third Year

Morning Session moved from the large room in the Stone Building to a larger room in the new addition (which we "creatively" named "the Wooden Building"). Here all 35 of us could sit in at least an oval, if not a circle. Mildred taught music to various groups in the Stone Building where I would sometimes accompany

---

[72] From the late summer 1975 newspaper article that ended Chapter II.

them with a harmonium brought back from a trip to India. While the level playground was mostly hard-packed dirt, students (and staff) were now able to play field games on campus. Early that year the school acquired a whiffle ball and a set of plastic hockey sticks — yellow and red — and so began the SBS version of "field hockey" that carries on at the Upper Building today.

Field hockey and skating on the Upper Building playground

Volunteers designed and built the first wooden play structure which students used so much it needed to be replaced after a few years.[73] On rainy days we had more room to square dance in the Wooden Building. In the winter we flooded the field to make ice, and almost every student learned to skate.

For Valentine's Day that year I created a card that featured each student out on the ice. Inspired by the old nursery rhyme about the woman and her many children who lived in a shoe, my drawing included a school housed in a hockey skate with a caricature of all the students engaged in various ice-time activities. While the mimeographed card faded long ago neither the memory of it nor the aroma of the mimeograph machine has!

---

[73] Designed and built by Jonas Gerard and Fletcher Lokey.

Faded 1976 Valentine's Day cartoon featuring every student attending SBS

Going into my third year of teaching language arts and math to 1st graders I was excited to be teaching a class of ten. We met in the larger of the two upstairs rooms in the Wooden Building, using various configurations of three tables that easily seated four or five at each. This allowed us a good deal of open floor space for students to work in small groups or pairs and gather in a circle to practice their Open Court drills. The class was lively and fun, the pace was rapid, and students made good progress as we rolled along. At this time we were very fortunate to have the assistance of Judy Shannon, a talented Satsangi educator from the West Coast, who spent several weeks volunteering in the school. This eased the adjustment to what was, for me, a "large" class of first-year students. Judy went on to head a school connected to Sant Ji's ashram near Vancouver, Canada.[74]

The adjoining room was used for math and social studies and the large landing outside held a table with chairs for small high school classes. Mildred began to teach French while I taught Spanish, so nooks and corners were found for the variety of classes that were going on simultaneously. The day-to-day life of the school seemed considerably busier than during the first two years, a feeling which no doubt came from being more driven by a tight schedule.

---

[74] In the spring of 2018, Judy shared these thoughts about her time at SBS: "I am very grateful to Kent for allowing me to spend several weeks at Sant Bani School in 1975, when I was just beginning my teaching career. I was impressed with both the warm atmosphere and how inspirational every element of the school was. Whether listening to the powerful stories at the beginning of the day or attending a reading lesson, every moment was spent in a meaningful way. Each child was keenly absorbed in the curriculum and the interaction between teachers and students was unlike anything I had observed in a typical school setting. The children were excited about learning while being nurtured and encouraged. At the same time, I was amazed to see the elaborate planning that went into the Open Court Language Arts classes. While the lessons were captivating and learning took place in a seamless manner, behind everything was a detailed, highly organized approach. The inspiration that I gained at Sant Bani carried over to my teaching career. For example, I used the Open Court Program for both the primary and intermediate students at Kirpal Ashram School in Surrey, British Columbia. All the children made significant progress, and their transformations were exciting to witness over time. Sant Bani School is an oasis of love, of true education encompassing all children and their unique needs."

An Outside Perspective

Peace Prevails at Sant Bani School
by Charles McDonald
Laconia Evening Citizen, October 29, 1975

SANBORNTON – The school buildings are hidden up on a hill off Knox Mt. Road and a visitor will find no sign, save a small varnished wooden plank with the words "Sant Bani Ashram" emblazoned under a rising sun at the head of the road. After a short hike up a rocky path, past a well-tended vegetable garden and through some trees, a stained-glass swan rises next to the door of a comfortable, sturdy stone building. It is the Sant Bani Ashram School, and the sound of happy children greets you before the doors have opened.

The school is a privately operated elementary facility with a ninth grade, part of a hoped-for secondary wing, and it has more applications for admission than it can handle. Why do parents spend hard earned money to send their children to a small, two-year old facility that boasts no special federal or state grants?

"We think it offers an alternative from the public schools," Kent Bicknell, principal of the school says. "The reaction of many visitors is to notice the peace and trust the children have toward each other. They don't feel anyone is going to pull any tricks on them, and most visitors are amazed at how well they all get along." The school is the only one in the country associated with the Sant Bani spiritual community, a meditative group composed of disciples of Kirpal Singh, an Indian Sikh who died in 1974 after approving the idea of a school at his disciples' Ashram (community). Master Kirpal Singh, a saint, traveled to the hills of Sanbornton to found the Ashram in 1963. No more disciples can join the community, since initiation ceased with the founder's death.

There are 30 children in the school, about half of whom are offspring of Sant Bani disciples... The central theme of the community [the Ashram] is that God is in all people. "Kirpal Singh taught that this was found in all faiths, and our lives are a progress toward a union with God," Bicknell explained.

The young principal, a candidate for a doctoral degree in curriculum development, currently spends one day a week at Boston University. Three teachers, all with backgrounds in various academic pursuits, provide what the principal feels is a strong academic background in languages, reading, the arts, English, grammar and mathematics.

The children must bring a vegetarian lunch to the school, a reflection of the strict vegetarian diet of the disciples of Kirpal Singh. Other than an unstructured meditation period in the morning, children are not required to partake in any spiritual exercises of the community. "One thing we're very set on is not to undo any child's faith," Mr. Bicknell says. He points out that moral and ethical lessons throughout the school day may be drawn from holy figures spanning all religions of the world. The school day, which runs from 8:15 a.m. to 3:15 p.m., takes place in a modified open classroom structure. "I'm not opposed to the traditional concept of education, and here children have a certain subject taught at a certain period every day. But if the child brings something to class that is interesting, we may stop what we're doing and discuss it," said Bicknell.

The tuition rate is $500 per year, but the school will not turn away children whose parents may be hard-pressed financially. The school, completed last September, was built with volunteer labor from the community, and day-to-day operations are subsidized by donations from "100 or so" disciples of Kirpal Singh throughout the country.

This year a wing was completed for the secondary program, and Mr. Bicknell hopes to add a grade a year until the school, certified by the state, is complete. He is also hoping to have 50 per cent of the school's operating costs, estimated at $1100 per pupil, paid for out of tuition.

The school is open to new ideas, and Mr. Bicknell finds himself addressing community groups in surrounding towns. Workshops have been conducted with teachers visiting from public schools.

How far is the new school going? The principal said he is not trying to drum up new students, and he would hope for a total of 50 when all grades are completed. As with any school principal, he worries about where the equipment for more sophisticated secondary school classes will come from. "Everyone has been involved in this school from the top down," Bicknell said. "We don't intend to become a large community... but it's become very exciting."

The article was accompanied by two photos with the following captions:

ROBERT SCHONGALLA, a teacher at the Sant Bani Ashram School in Sanbornton, is surrounded by pupils on the playing field behind the school building. Subject at the time was the travel of the sun across the sky and its relation to time. A "shadow stick" to chart sun movement is in the foreground.

ERIC PERKINS displays the leopard he printed from a carved block of linoleum at the Sant Bani Ashram School in Sanbornton. Block printing is one of the crafts which supplement a strong academic structure at the 30-student private school.

One of the new wrinkles that came with two buildings was how to be sure the spaces were cleaned on a regular basis. Karen and I were, of course, happy to keep our home in order the first year, and in the second year the teachers were able to do the same for the Stone Building. Expecting teachers to continue cleaning all the spaces was too much, however, so we implemented a plan where families helped on a rotating basis. Over the course of the year every family had four or five weekends when they were responsible for an in-depth cleaning of a section of the facilities. Mildred and I agreed that asking all families to share the load was in harmony with the school's culture and were pleased that it provided students an opportunity to do more than happened in their daily tasks. Though not without its challenges, this feature became a part of the SBS fabric.

As the ship of the school sailed through the winter, interest in us from outside parties continued to grow. Midway through the year a student applied to 8th grade who had been struggling with a number of issues in relation to school. She and her parents toured the school and were thrilled with what they saw. We were happy to admit her as we thought she would thrive in a different environment. It soon became apparent, however, that what was driving her was a need to rebel against whatever system she was in. As the year progressed she not only resisted the efforts the faculty made on her behalf but she consistently tried to draw other students into her "island of discontent." We worked with the student and her parents to chart an alternate course, but by the next fall it was clear that our high school program was not a good fit for what she needed.

I recalled my conversation with Miss Sati, the principal at the school in India, about the boy who was dismissed because he was "polluting the atmosphere," and, quaint as that may sound, it accurately describes the impact of this student on the school. I remember well the phone call I made to her parents informing them that their daughter could no longer attend SBS; while they were understanding and supportive, I hung up the phone and burst into tears. It was a powerful lesson for all of the adults that SBS should not try to be all things for all students.

Word-of-mouth continued to be our best endorsement, and it looked like more students would be enrolling for the fourth year, 1976-77. We created a high school application as the need to screen applicants became apparent. An early version of that application provides a clear picture of the high school from a student perspective. Quoting two "current" students it asks a series of questions for the adolescent applicant to consider before coming to SBS:

> Please read the following comments by present high school students. Think about each comment carefully, and answer the questions which follow.
>
> "Before you attend the school you should know that it is a very special place... The atmosphere is quite peaceful and friendly in general, and after you have attended for a few days you will realize that rough language and deeds feel strangely out of place."
>
> "It might be hard for someone coming in from a larger school to adjust to the size of the school and the amount of responsibility each student carries. Unless a student is willing to work hard and adjust to the different atmosphere, he or she won't benefit from the advantages of the school."
>
> - Do you enjoy small learning groups?
> - How do you feel you could benefit from this school?
> - Can you accept the understanding that the school exists for the good of everyone in it, and that you should be looking for ways in which to contribute?
> - Do you feel that you have any special problems? If so, describe them and how you feel the school might help with them.
> - How do you get along with: 1) younger children; 2) peers; 3) adults?

It was apparent that SBS was a "very special place" and the experience with the student who did not fit underscored that. It was also clear that students were thriving in what was, on reflection, an environment that embodied pedagogical characteristics of the "progressive education" movement. While we did not set out to emulate the models inspired by Bronson Alcott, John Dewey and others, the combination of the teachings of Master Kirpal Singh (with emphasis on the value of each individual as well as the guidelines embodied in "Toward the New Education") and the backgrounds of the faculty helped create a warm environment that supported each child. Given these ingredients, SBS manifested almost all the markers of a progressive education as outlined in Wikipedia:

1. Emphasis on learning by doing—hands-on projects, expeditionary learning, experiential learning
2. Integrated curriculum focused on thematic units
3. Integration of entrepreneurship into education
4. Strong emphasis on problem solving and critical thinking
5. Group work and development of social skills
6. Understanding and action as the goals of learning as opposed to rote knowledge
7. Collaborative and cooperative learning projects
8. Education for social responsibility and democracy
9. Highly personalized learning accounting for each individual's personal goals
10. Integration of community service and service learning projects into the daily curriculum
11. Selection of subject content by looking forward to ask what skills will be needed in future society
12. De-emphasis on textbooks in favor of varied learning resources
13. Emphasis on lifelong learning and social skills
14. Assessment by evaluation of child's projects and productions[75]

---

[75] "**Progressive education** is a pedagogical movement that began in the late nineteenth century; it has persisted in various forms to the present. The term *progressive* was engaged to distinguish this education from the traditional Euro-American curricula of the 19th century, which was rooted in classical preparation for the university and strongly differentiated by social class. By contrast, progressive education finds its roots in present experience. Most progressive education programs have these qualities in common."
https://en.wikipedia.org/wiki/Progressive_education
The 14 qualities shared above line up nicely with the current Mission and Values of SBS: http://www.santbani.org/meet/mission/. See Chapter VI.

As the year turned from 1975 to 1976 those of us who first dreamt of a school at the ashram were amazed and delighted by how fast it was happening.

The Coming of Sant Ajaib Singh,
Successor to Master Kirpal Singh

The Satsangis living at or near the ashram continued to practice the spiritual path taught by Master Kirpal Singh at the same time that we missed his physical presence on so many levels. The value of spending time in the company of an enlightened soul is a matter of experience that cannot be conveyed in words. In India and the U.S. various successors had emerged to carry on the spiritual teachings, but none of them worked for those of us at the ashram. Understandably this was a period of longing and uncertainty that, at times, edged toward despair.

Russell and Judith Perkins, who were so instrumental in founding the ashram and the school, felt keenly the absence of Master Kirpal in human form. Russell had served as Master Kirpal Singh's representative for many years and as editor of the monthly magazine *Sat Sandesh,* and both he and Judith had had a lot of personal contact with the Master. In early February of 1976 Russell received an inner order from Master Kirpal Singh to travel to India to find his successor. Russell describes in detail the saga of this 20th century adventure in his terrific book, *Impact of a Saint.* He begins:

> Even as I despaired, the first intimation of the Master's coming came in the form of a letter from a Colombian radiologist, a distinguished and respected initiate of Kirpal Singh, then in his fifties, who told his daughter and son-in-law (both good friends of mine, who lived near the Ashram) that Master Kirpal had told him within that Ajaib Singh was almost ready to come forth.
>
> Then, about the time of Kirpal Singh's birthday (February 6) 1976, the Master ordered me, from within, to go to Rajasthan and find Ajaib Singh. I did not want to go. I was afraid. But no appeal was possible and no peace did I have until I had bought my ticket.[76]

---

[76] Russell Perkins, *Impact of a Saint* (1980; 2nd printing 1989), p. 149.

Russell went to India and found, as he states, "his old friend (Master Kirpal) in a new suit (Sant Ajaib Singh)." I recorded the impact of this discovery in my book, *Rainbow On My Heart (ROMH)*:

> After an arduous journey with many roadblocks he suc-
> ceeded in finding Sant Ajaib Singh (Sant Ji) in the rural village of
> 77 RB in the desert province of Rajasthan. Russell sent us a cable
> that said, "HAVE FOUND AJAIB SINGH – HE IS REAL – WE
> LOVE HIM" and we were giddy with excitement and anticipa-
> tion. After months of confusion, this felt clear and right. Russell
> spent a few hours with Sant Ji, and then in March a group of three
> visited Him and spent the night. They brought back similar testi-
> mony as to the quality of Sant Ji and His Life.[77]

From the moment I read Russell's telegram I experienced a burning desire to meet Sant Ji that grew so strong I knew I had to travel to India as soon as possible. Again, from *ROMH*:

> By the time I was ready to leave, two more from Sant Bani
> Ashram were also ready — Robert and Wendy Schongalla. Robert
> was teaching at Sant Bani School and Wendy was helping at the
> Ashram — as they both do today… We left for Delhi and arrived
> on the morning of Thursday, April 1st, 1976.[78]

The story of Robert, Wendy, Raaj Kumar Bagga[79] and my journey to Village 77RB in the desert of Rajasthan and our six-day stay
with Sant Ji and the villagers seems as magical today as when it
happened over forty years ago. During the second day of our visit
I asked Sant Ji if he would visit SBS when he came to the U.S. He
responded, "How could I not come? Heart speaks to heart. How
can I refuse your love?" On our last day Sant Ji reiterated that he

---

[77] *Rainbow On My Heart: A Memoir of the Early Years of the Mission of Sant Ajaib Singh* by Kent Bicknell (2002), p. 1. This memoir has a good deal of information about Sant Ji's relation to SBS, not all of which is captured in this history of the founda-tion of the school. *ROMH* was written using a combination of personal journals (written and taped), published articles and memory. It provides a detailed account of the beginning years of Sant Ji's mission (1976-1979) from the perspective of a follower of Sant Mat (me), who was fortunate enough to spend a good deal of time with Sant Ji.

[78] *ROMH*, p. 2.

[79] Raaj Kumar Bagga (or "Pappu" as he was affectionately known) served as Sant Ji's translator from this trip through the remainder of Sant Ji's physical life.

would be glad to see us in the school. I asked if he had a message for the students and he said, "I send my love to all. Love is the true *sandesh* (message)," adding that he would meet them all when he came.[80] A year later Sant Ji came to the U.S. and met everyone during his initial month-long stay at Sant Bani Ashram. He saw individual students and their families, visited the school in session and, on May 11, 1977, gave a talk to the school community.[81]

Finishing Year Three in Style:
Antoine de Saint-Exupéry's *The Little Prince*

All of the initiates connected to Sant Bani were thrilled to have an answer to the question of who would carry on the spiritual work of the ashram: Sant Ajaib Singh, Master Kirpal's best student! I returned from India with a new spring in my step and was eager to plunge back into the daily life of SBS.

One of the first items on the agenda, however, was to get through the glorious/notorious spring epoch known as "mud season." It really is true that owing to its location SBS has had to call off school on occasion owing to the mud in the road being axle-deep. In the first couple of decades the dirt road was much longer, stretching a mile and a half from the junction of Knox Mountain Road up and down the "seven hills"[82] to the campus. The ashram tractor helped extricate stranded automobiles on a regular basis, and with a combination of calling off school, skilled work by the town road agent and his crew and the inevitable thawing of the deep freeze, survive we did!

---

[80] *ROMH*, pp. 15 and 45.

[81] This talk, in which Sant Ji stressed the importance of education as "the center stone for the foundation" of our lives, is published in Chapter IV. Both *ROMH* and the next chapter in this book have more about Sant Ji's visit to SBS in the spring of 1977. A movie that captures a few minutes of his visit to the school is available at https://santbaniashram.org/videos-of-the-master/. Scroll down to "Sant Ajaib Singh 1977 Visit to Sant Bani School."

[82] The ashram and school's neighbor and long-time friend, Davey Sanville, once told me there were seven hills between Knox Mountain Road and his house at the end of Osgood Road, a journey he walked almost every day as he went back and forth to work at the Webster Valve Company in Franklin, New Hampshire.

With 30+ students in the school we were excited about the possibility of finishing the year with a grander production than *St. Jerome and the Lion* had been the spring before. When Mildred suggested an adaptation of *The Little Prince*, Antoine de Saint-Exupéry's wondrous story, I wholeheartedly agreed that it would be great to present it to a live audience. Published in 1943, *The Little Prince* proved to be a classic.[83] The childlike perspective of the prince, a visitor from a small planet where he is the sole inhabitant, is revealed through an extended conversation with a solo pilot whose plane went down in the desert. Page after page is illustrated by delightful watercolors that are as unforgettable in their simplicity as the many lessons shared throughout the narrative. The freshness of the insights shine through as brightly today as when I first read it in the 1960s.

Like so many before and after, my generation loved the prince and identified with his frustration, concern and puzzlement over many of the adults who appear in the book, strawmen though they were. As he visited different planets he found a king who ruled over nothing while thinking he ruled everything, a conceited man who considered all others his admirers, a businessman who said he owned the stars because he was the first one to think of counting them all, and a geographer who only recorded things rather than explore. Dramatizing *The Little Prince* seemed like a perfect way to bring Year Three to a close.

A stage was built in the lower level of the Stone Building, costumes and scenery were created and Mildred began to block the play after parts were cast and lines memorized. Roles included Bethany as the Little Prince, her older sister Heather as the Rose, Eric as the Pilot, Gina as the Fox, Suzi as the Snake, Thomas as one of the live Volcanoes and Peter as the Lamplighter. Before casting Elaina as the Tippler, Mildred and I discussed at some length the wisdom of presenting an alcoholic (who drinks to forget his shame that comes about because he drinks too much) to our elementary age audience and their parents. We decided that the value of the lesson was worth any concern that parents might have, and so Elaina gave a wonderful performance as a tipsy tippler.

---

[83] According to Wikipedia *The Little Prince* continues to sell over 2 million copies annually.

The entire student body was involved in bringing the adaptation to life and the impact was powerful. Lessons within the story were learned as students made the dialogue their own. Three-quarters of the way through the play the Fox explains to the Little Prince (after an extended interaction in which she helps him understand what it means to be a friend), *"And now here is my secret, a very simple secret: It is only with the heart that one can see rightly; what is essential is invisible to the eye."* As that line was delivered in rehearsal after rehearsal and then to a live audience, I smiled at the parallel wisdom found in that little unsigned note I had taped the year before to a wooden column facing the stage: *"I love you. But who are you?"*

Trust (even blind trust at times), kindness, confidence, support, laughter, risk-taking, courage and all-around growth were the visible and invisible fruits developing in the SBS greenhouse. As Master Kirpal wrote in "Toward the New Education," *"The chief malady of current education is that it results in the disassociation of heart and head. It lays emphasis on the development of head, and does sharpen the intellect to some extent. But more essential is the liberation of the heart. That will be done when the reason is awakened in sympathy for the poor, the weak and the needy. Sacrifice grows out of the heart, so the heart is required to be unfolded."* Over and over again the hearts of students, staff, parents and the audience were "unfolded" through the timeless values shared in our production of *The Little Prince*.

At the same time that hearts were unfolding the teachers and I were pleased with the academic growth we measured across all the grades. Interest in the school as a dynamic alternative continued to grow and the prospect of adding more students and staff was exciting even if somewhat daunting. While the plan had been to add one high school grade a year, over the summer we added two more years. Carolyn skipped from 9th to 11th and was joined by Sanbornton residents Melissa, Evelyn and Steve who became the first class to graduate from the high school in 1978. Eric and Gina became sophomores, and Andrea and Scott advanced to 9th. This meant adding more courses, as teaching grades 9, 10 and 11 would be very different than teaching three 9th graders.

Since there were no summer building projects there was time to develop a more complex schedule that would accommodate everything. As we worked to juggle competing demands it was easy to see why educators would sometimes lament that "Demon Schedule" seemed to drive everything—a concern I continued to hear as I came to know more and more heads of schools. We had hoped that Sant Ajaib Singh would come for a visit during the summer, but that was not to be as his first visit to America was postponed until the following spring.[84] I made a short trip to India in August where I spent several days with Sant Ji and the Bagga family in New Delhi, and learned enough Hindi that I began to send and receive letters from Sant Ji in the Devanagari script.

The wise Richmond Mayo-Smith[85] once shared with me that for school people summer is like a weekend: June feels like Friday; July is Saturday; and August is Sunday. "Sunday" evening came and we were all eager to start our fourth year when Monday dawned in early September.

---

[84] See *ROMH*, Chapter II for the story of the 1976 summer visit that was not to be.
[85] Richmond was a grandparent of two SBS students, a veteran of independent schools, and a trustee. See the end of the Introduction for more on Richmond.

Chapter IV: The Fourth Year (1976-77)
Keeping the Balance

Elementary Schedule (1-8) – Fall 1976

Grade	1st	2nd	3rd	4th-5th	6th-7th-8th
8:15-8:45	Morning Session				
8:50-9:50	Boni	L.A.* w/Kent	L.A. w/Robert	L.A. w/Debbie	L.A. w/Mildred
10:15-11:10	Boni	Block** w/Kent	Block w/Debbie	Block w/Mildred	Geography w/Russell
11:15-12	Boni	Math w/Kent & Kim	Math w/Debbie		Math w/Fletcher
12-12:10	Reading				
12:10-1:10	Lunch + Recess				
1:10-1:30	Independent Reading				
1:30-2	Boni	Music***			
2-3	Out	Art w/Boni			
3-3:15	Clean Up				

*L.A. = Language Arts (reading, writing, spelling, grammar, *et al*)
**Block = where social studies and science lessons rotated
***Music was singing or recorder, taught by different teachers

High School Schedule (9-11) – Fall 1976

Grade	9th	10th	11th
8:15-8:45	Morning Session		
8:50-9:50	World History w/Russell		
10:10-11:10	Earth Science w/Robert	Algebra II w/Fletcher	
11:15-12:15	English I w/Robert	English II & III w/Mildred & Russell	
12:15-1	Lunch + Recess		
1-2	Algebra I w/Gerald	French II w/Robert Spanish II, III w/Kent	
2-3	Spanish I w/Debbie	Biology w/Ann	Independent Study
3-3:15	Clean Up		

More Growth

In the mid-1970s there was a growing interest in alternative opportunities for schooling in central New Hampshire, and different places invited me to speak about Sant Bani. New people, including teachers from other schools, were coming to see SBS in action,[86] and as word spread, several forces converged. Local families were intrigued, siblings of current students wanted to come, and Satsangis from around the country relocated to be near the ashram and send their children to SBS. While we were no longer surprised by the growth it was none-the-less exciting to open Year Four with 45 students, including four in the 11th grade.[87]

As the complexity of course offerings increased, we added another full-time staff member, Boni Teed, as well as more part-time teachers. Ann Matty returned to teach biology and Kim Ilowit came to tutor students in the younger grades. We were extremely fortunate that Fletcher Lokey, a Satsangi who graduated from Dartmouth College and lived at the ashram, was willing to teach math at the junior high and high school level. Our "veteran" teachers, Mildred, Robert, Debbie, Gerald and Russell, were happy about the growth and ready to provide more offerings, as captured in the schedule above.

The advent of Sant Ajaib Singh (Sant Ji) continued to provide a lift for all of the Satsangis who were drawn to him. This impacted both the ashram and the school, especially since Sant Ji designated Sant Bani Ashram as his headquarters in North America. That meant, among other things, that both the monthly trips to India to spend time in meditation with him and the details of his upcoming world tour were coordinated by Judith Perkins and the ashram

---

[86] For example, on April 23, 1976, I received a letter from a teacher at Sandwich Central School who requested to come visit SBS with two colleagues after hearing a presentation I made to elementary school teachers in Meredith. The three teachers spent the day with us on May 12, 1976.

[87] The 45 included: Mary, Mary, Jamie, David, Rachel and Kira in 1st; Chris, Per, Paul, Faith, Leah, Becky, Mike, Christina, Corey and Kara in 2nd; Todd, Mira, Leanne and Claudia in 3rd; Bev, Ben, Bethany, Jason and Samantha in 4th; Thomas, Linda, Jenny, Natalie and Dean in 5th; Geri in 6th; Heather, Elaina and Billy in 7th; Suzi and Peter in 8th; Andrea, Scott and Lisa in 9th; Eric and Gina in 10th; and Carolyn, Evelyn, Melissa and Stephen in 11th. This is the last year all the students will be listed.

staff. Interest in the ashram grew, and more Satsangis around the country made plans to move to central New Hampshire. When it was announced that Sant Ji would be spending the month of May 1977 in residence at the ashram, those numbers increased.

In October I sent Sant Ji a packet of drawings and messages from a group of SBS students and he responded with what was to be the first of many messages to students at the school:

7th Oct. 1976

My Dear Children of Sant Bani Ashram School,
    I send His Love and Greetings to you. I appreciate your love, which I have received through your drawings. Dear Children of Light, be obedient to your teachers and faithful to your parents.
    The initiated children are advised to put more love in their practices, and keep close to Him. Non-initiated are advised to have Godly thoughts. Love all. Remember, Love is God, and God is Love.
I love you all. With All His Love,
Yours affectionately,
Ajaib Singh[88]

Sant Ji's request that students obey their teachers was a theme he sounded frequently. As he made clear time and again, the purpose of education was to provide the building blocks — the foundation — for a child's life so that she or he might have a bright future. Speaking to some initiates who wished to found a school in California, Sant Ji said, "*This school will be for the children. In this school the lives of the children will be made and they will be given that education, that knowledge, which will make their career and which will make them stand on their feet when they grow up... and that teaching, that education, should not be different than the education that other children get in the world.*"[89]

---

[88] *ROMH*, p. 87. Sant Ji's citations of "His Love" refer to the love coming from his spiritual teacher, Master Kirpal Singh.

[89] Excerpt from a talk Sant Ji gave in 1985 to a group of Satsangis in Ukiah, CA. See also the talk Sant Ji gave to the SBS community during his visit in May of 1977 (Chapter IV). In July of 1980, on his second visit to Sant Bani, Sant Ji addressed the school community and said, "*We know that the most important thing for every child in the building of his educated life is school. It is the stepping-stone of the life of the children, so if the school is good and if the teachers are good, only then can the children get good education from the very beginning. When they grow older and go to college they will be*

The Middle Way: Balancing Competing Interests

Sant Ji's explicit statement that education at a school founded by Satsangis should match what other children in the world were getting reiterates the vision of Master Kirpal Singh as well: Sant Bani School should be an inclusive educational institution committed to strong academics and character development. SBS always welcomed students and families of any belief system, of any religious (or non-religious) background or culture, and over the decades we have hosted students, families and teachers from a range that includes atheists, agnostics, Christians, Muslims, Hindus, Jews, Buddhists, Pagans and others.

At the same time, a primary reason for founding SBS was to support the values of Satsangis: values in apparent opposition to the prevailing culture of 1970s America. Satsangis adopted a lifestyle that featured an enlightened spiritual teacher from India; a vegetarian diet that prohibited the use of tobacco, alcohol or drugs; at least two hours of meditation each day; and the earning of one's own livelihood so as not to be dependent on others. Maintaining the balance between supporting this set of values and being open and inclusive was not always easy, and with our expanding population it was inevitable that differences of opinion arose as to where the "middle way" lay. As the number of stakeholders increased, what had been a relatively simple conversation amongst a few like-minded educators[90] grew in complexity and the school received lots of advice as to how we should operate and what should be in the curriculum. For example, it was proposed that:

- SBS should not have competitive athletics as it was not good for one team to "win" at the expense of another team's loss
- SBS should not offer drama because it was not helpful for a student's budding ego to stand in front of an audience and

---

able to understand things much better." (July 13, 1980, "Education and Discipline," Sant Ajaib Singh to the SBS Community; see Appendix).

[90] E.g., as in the first year when the family did not want their child subjected to any kind of formal evaluation as they felt that "testing" was what had spoiled their own education. I was able to reassure them that any tests would be used for diagnostic purposes to help improve the curriculum (see Chapter I).

receive applause with the end result being pride (rather than humility)

- SBS should not host dances since it was not healthy for adolescents to have such close physical contact with each other
- English Class should not read literature such as Shakespeare as the Bard was too bawdy and suggestive for developing minds; at the same time no "gloomy" literature should be read since there was an abundance of "cheerful" literature to choose from
- Teachers should monitor student lunches on a regular basis to be sure that they were not only vegetarian but also composed of organic, non-processed foods
- SBS should stop allowing students to call teachers by their first names as respect could not be taught under conditions of such familiarity
- The Head of School should "march" everyone, students and faculty alike, to the Satsang Hall every day and have them sit in meditation for an hour
- Teachers should not assign homework as Satsangi parents wanted their children to have time for spiritual practices at home rather than spending time on schoolwork (which should be done in school), and non-Satsangi parents wanted their children to be free to do chores and have family time
- SBS should make only families receiving financial aid clean a section of the school on the weekend, as families paying full tuition should be exempt

While a few of these were brought to Sant Ji for guidance, the majority were sorted out by the faculty. In retrospect, it seems as if everyone who came to the ashram and/or the school, whether a Satsangi or not, was in the midst of figuring out how best to create a healthy future for people everywhere. We were all on a search that included reassessing our childhoods, particularly around schooling, to better understand what had worked for us and what had not. That being said, most of the suggestions for how we should change our operation came from a handful of Satsangis.

When people adopt a way of life very different from how they were raised it can happen that aspects of "fundamentalism" crop up for support. As the great Indian sage Sri Ramakrishna (1836-

1886) described it, a young sapling needs a fence to protect it from wandering cows who would eat its tender shoots. Later, when the sapling has matured into a full-grown tree, it provides shade and shelter for cows.[91] In striving to live the teachings of Sant Mat every day it was sometimes easy to build a protective fence around the spiritual practices, and that fence was often based on duality: something was either right or wrong; good or bad. Balance and moderation could be viewed as compromising core values, or even "selling out."

Almost all of the Satsangis involved in SBS in those first years, teachers and parents alike, were relative newcomers to Sant Mat. Russell and Judith Perkins were not, however, as they had been living this way of life for fifteen years prior to the founding of Sant Bani School. In Russell's role as head of the ashram his advice was sought by Satsangis across the country; in his role as a teacher at SBS, Satsangi parents and others looked to him for guidance. In 1976 Sant Ji had asked Russell to be his representative in North America and to edit a new monthly publication, *Sant Bani Magazine*. With his already long-established connection to Master Kirpal, Russell was in a great position to provide wise council to those interested in all aspects of a spiritual path, and the school was very fortunate to have him on the staff.

What Russell Perkins Brought to Sant Bani School

In 1991 Sant Ji shared these thoughts: *"In the school we do not want to impose our ideologies on the children. Since we are living in this world, and because this world keeps changing, so we have to go along with this world. I hope that you will understand that it is very important for us to keep making changes according to the requirement of society and the present situation of the world."*[92]

This approach mirrors exactly what Russell brought to SBS. While his background was rich and his world view well-established, he did not impose his way of thinking on anyone. Rather, he

---

[91] E.g., from *The Gospel of Sri Ramakrishna*, Chapter 18: *"Spiritual discipline is necessary. When the Aśwattha tree is a mere sapling, it must be enclosed by a fence; otherwise the cattle will eat it. But the fence may be taken away when the trunk grows thick and strong. Then even an elephant tied to the tree cannot harm it."*
[92] Excerpt from a 1991 letter that Sant Ji wrote to a school teacher in Massachusetts.

listened with care, attending to each student on the basis that each mattered. Among Russell's many contributions to the foundation of SBS was a tireless championing of the worth of each individual supported by a broad but deep understanding of spirituality. These two traits were continually reinforced by an almost encyclopedic knowledge of the humanities. For Russell, love and inclusion lay at the very heart of education. Given how critical his role was in helping build the foundation of SBS, I asked his younger sister, Helen, to share her perspective on Russell's childhood and beyond.

Russell, My Dear Big Brother
by Helen Perkins

Who is this "Renaissance man," Russell Perkins, and what were the influences in his own life? Though many salient events of his background and upbringing are recounted in his first book, *Impact of a Saint*, and in his most recent memoir, *Stumbling Toward God*, still, as his sister who had the good fortune to grow up with him, being two years his junior, I would like to add my own input.

Though a New Englander through and through, Russell was born in Tampa, Florida, in March 1935, the first of four children. Soon after his birth, our parents returned to Beverly, Massachusetts, where they both had grown up. They were very young, very much in love, and, to our great benefit, totally into parenting.

Because reading and books were important to them, they passed this love on to us, and both Russell's and my earliest memories center around the stories (bed-time and often day-time!) that were read to us. These were books that we loved, pored over, heard Mother and Dad read to us over and over again. Many of those stories, wisely chosen, sank deeply into our hearts and affected us profoundly.

Anyone who knows Russell undoubtedly knows of his love for the book and movie, *The Wizard of Oz*. As a child our mother owned one of the earliest editions of the book (then entitled *The Wonderful Wizard of Oz*) as well as its immediate sequel, *The Marvelous Land of Oz*. She loved both books and, recognizing Russell's keen interest and his obviously quick grasp of ideas, language, and verbal expression from an early age, she shared with him the book she loved so much. Mother also enjoyed going to the movies (a love that her son happily inherited!), and when in 1939 the magnificent film of *The Wizard of Oz* came to the local Ware theater in Beverly, she carefully prepared him for it. He was four years old,

and it profoundly touched him in a way that is inconceivable —
perhaps stirring in his soul memories of some now-forgotten
longing, resonating in the unforgettable line, "There's no place
like home." This life-long love affair with the film, which Russell
has viewed perhaps more than fifty times, had its culmination
when Sant Bani School produced *The Wizard of Oz: A Musical Play
in Nine Scenes* in 1978. It was adapted by Russell from L. Frank
Baum's book and the movie, and directed by Mildred Meeh, with
a large cast of Sant Bani students. A memorable event. Four years
later, in 1982, the school produced *The Marvelous Land of Oz*, with
lyrics by Russell who also, along with Mildred Meeh, directed it.
This was an equally memorable event.

That Russell was a "natural" for directing and scripting *The
Wizard of Oz* (and other plays) should come as no surprise; not
only for his love of that book, but also for his keen interest in the
dramatic arts, both play-writing and acting. This manifested as
early as his sophomore year at Tilton-Northfield High School with
his lead role in the senior play, *January Thaw*. The same year saw
him, again as the lead, in the Harmony Grange of Sanbornton's
production of *Peck's Bad Boy*. His acting as Hennery Peck elicited
a comment from a local newspaper covering the play, "It's hard
to know where Peck's bad boy leaves off, and Russell Perkins begins."

In his junior year he performed in Gilbert & Sullivan's *The
Mikado* as Pooh-Bah (the Lord High Everything Else), as well a
number of other plays. This intense interest, though dormant during his late teen "evangelical years," rose again after he left Gordon College, where he had been studying for the ministry, and
enrolled in Boston University's new Division of Theatre Arts. The
experience, skills and knowledge Russell absorbed in those two
dynamic years studying theater arts would be shared with students and colleagues for years to come.

Another deep and life-long influence for us both were the
Thornton Burgess bird and animal stories, which both Mother and
Dad had had as children, and they quite naturally passed their
love of them on to us. Implicit in those books were the deep em-
pathy, respect, and compassion for animals and all living creatures, a concept that easily translated into our later embrace of
both non-violence toward animals and vegetarianism. We learned
our birds and animals early on from these books.

Russell's penchant for absorbing information about the natural world was epitomized in three large volumes: the beautifully
illustrated *Audubon's Birds of America*, *Mammals of the World*, and

Birds of North America. At age 8 or 9, he saved the quarters that he earned each Saturday by helping Dad on his Cushman bakery delivery route, bought these huge books, and then began memorizing the phyla, class, order, family, genus, and species of each animal or bird. I tried to keep up with him, but when he started in on fish in another book, I begged out![93]

This ability to easily memorize and retain what he read was a great asset in his later teaching, both at the school and in his Satsangs, drawing together many ideas, quotations, and historical facts, often injected with a great sense of humor as an added bonus.

With his insatiable reading and wide-ranging taste in books, the desire and aptitude for writing followed naturally. When he was nine, one of his Christmas presents was a portable Smith-Corona typewriter, on which he hunt-and-pecked his way to many stories, a published letter in *Child Life* magazine, and recaps and summaries of the Beverly City Club's basketball games, which were printed in the *Beverly Evening Times.* (Dad was the manager/coach of the team from 1946-1948 and Russell was his cub reporter and sports writer.) I have always thought of that typewriter as a foreshadowing of the future: an instrument paving the way to one of his later careers as a typesetter and printer, what to speak of his facility to express himself in the written word.

His high school yearbook (he graduated from the then Tilton-Northfield High School, now Winnisquam Regional High School, in 1952) noted this about Russell: *"Pious Russ... A yen for books and learning..."* Pithy and accurate.

That lifelong "yen for books and learning" also encompassed an early awareness of spiritual longing (which later in his teens, as noted above, took the form of embracing evangelical Christianity — hence the "pious Russ" sobriquet). We did go to Sunday School from an early age and attended the worship services, too, mainly at the First Baptist Church in Beverly. After coming home from these services, Russell, from about age five onward, would set up cushions or drag chairs into the living room, saying, "Let's play church." Though the cushions and chairs undoubtedly absorbed some of the gospel message, the main feature of "playing

---

[93] Memorization came easily, though, and the year we "discovered" Major League Baseball (1946, when the Red Sox ran away with the American League pennant, only to lose the World Series in seven games to the St. Louis Cardinals), we soaked up as much baseball lore and statistics as we could, memorizing batting averages, home runs, pitching records, and pennant winners back to 1901.

church" was Russell's preaching to his captive audience, his congregation of one: his patient and compliant sister.

This, too, like that typewriter, seemed to presage his later career as minister and synthesizer of Sant Mat and Christianity. Fast forward about 32 years: at the Unity of Man Conference in Delhi, February 1974, where in front of anywhere from 50,000–100,000 delegates and interested participants who were assembled from all over the world, Russell was asked to give a talk. Yes. On the stage with Master Kirpal and other notable dignitaries. And it all began with that congregation of one.[94]

His Sunday School teacher gave him a wonderful and influential paperback volume, *Pictures Stories from the Old Testament*. This was a comic-book format, beautifully illustrated. It raised the question in Russell's nine-year-old mind: "If God spoke so clearly to these prophets in the Old Testament, why can't He speak to us?" When he asked our mother about this, she replied, "Well, it isn't like that now." The next questions that naturally arose in Russell's mind were, "Well, why isn't it like that now? Why doesn't He speak to us like He used to?" That need to know, to understand, to find the truth about God and our human existence, stemmed in part from that book and that question. Why can't we also have that kind of communion with God? This was one of the precipitating factors that, consciously or unconsciously, led to Russell's subsequent search for the truth.

In April of 1948 our father decided to move from Beverly, Massachusetts, to Sanbornton, New Hampshire, in order to lead a more quiet rural life. This he hoped to accomplish by opening the only general store and gas pumps in the tiny town 25 miles north of Concord. Sanbornton, especially Sanbornton Square where we lived, in 1948 was an extremely conservative town, its iconic Congregational Church and Town Hall being the hub of religious and social activities. Dad set about to revitalize the town by holding square dances when the prosaic Grange meetings concluded, instigating a PTA, becoming town moderator, installing streetlights along the one road through the Square, coaching boys' and girls' basketball teams, and initiating many other activities. With all of that, plus Dad's gregarious personality and the pres-

---

[94] Though he dropped out of the ministerial studies at Gordon College, Russell's consuming interest in religious topics was brought to fruition thirty years later when in 1986 he earned a Master's degree in Theological Studies from Harvard Divinity School.

ence of the store (which both Russell and I worked in) the towns-people became well aware of these newcomers in their midst and generally accepted us.

I mention this as, fast-forwarding some 15 years, Russell and his wife Judith had bought a farmhouse on over 200 acres about six miles from where we grew up. By this time, as he has re-counted in his books, his and Judith's spiritual interests had been realized by being led to the living Master Kirpal Singh and had been initiated into the practice of Sant Mat. In October 1963 Rus-sell and Judith invited Master Kirpal, during His Second World Tour, to their new home, Sant Bani Farm, an acreage that had been uninhabited for over a generation. Master graciously accepted the invitation and, in that memorable evening talk at the Franklin Unitarian Church, referred to their home as "Sant Bani Ashram."

The rest, as they say, is history: with, at first, the slow growth of the ashram and its influence in the surrounding area, then the upsurge of spiritual seekers in the late 1960s, new buildings erected on the ashram to accommodate the expanding Satsang, the birth of Sant Bani Press in Tilton where Master Kirpal's books and the magazine *Sat Sandesh* were printed, Master Kirpal's last tour in 1972, when He spent five days at Sant Bani (a bungalow had been built especially for him), and along with this, the found-ing in 1973 of Sant Bani School.

Sanbornton has never been the same. As many local towns-people came to the Satsangs and were initiated, I've always felt that Master Kirpal laid the foundation for all this by allowing our family to settle in this ostensibly conservative town 15 years pre-viously, for us to be accepted and trusted by the townspeople, so that when this strange new "Hindu thing" (as some called it) sud-denly arrived in the midst of their peaceful, bucolic town, it was not from, so to speak, an outsider invading their land. Rather, we were a known quantity.

Russell's recently published *Stumbling Toward God* conveys in great depth his spiritual search, especially the discussion con-cerning his embracing, and later, rejection, of evangelical Christi-anity. The book is a beautiful, poignant, and triumphant answer to that question, in effect, that he put to our mother, "Why can't God speak to us now like He did to those Old Testament proph-ets?"

Among the many dedicated and passionate teachers who have given so much to the students at Sant Bani School, Russell will be remembered for all he gave, shared, and for how much he believed in the students that he compassionately taught. ❑

"Believing in the students we compassionately teach" was an initial hallmark of Sant Bani School that continues today. Every teacher from the earliest days through the present brings a sincerity of purpose that honors and nurtures each child as a discrete individual who is also part of a community whose members continually learn from each other. Educators at SBS strive to put into practice Master Kirpal Singh's teaching that *Each one of us is unique in his own way. There is a divine purpose behind the life of everyone who comes into the world; no one has been created for nothing. We have something to learn from everyone. This is the mystery of humility.*[95] This constant recognition of the value of "the other" is an essential component of what brings nobility to the profession in the hands of a consummate educator like Russell. His guidance was invaluable as SBS mapped out a middle way that successfully supported Satsangi values while providing each child a full educational experience.

As the school grew the faculty adopted a "full educational experience" that included Shakespeare, athletic teams, plays and musicals, challenging literature that allowed our students to experience things beyond their daily lives, processed food items (as long as they were vegetarian), homework as needed and the expectation that all families cleaned a section of the school on the weekend several times a year. We endorsed the wisdom of the 17th century proverb "all work and no play makes Jack a dull boy" as we saw that real learning happened when healthy doses of hard work, collaboration and laughter were in the mix. We understood that our role as educators was to provide students with, in Sant Ji's words, "the stepping stones" to help them build their lives,[96] and that the best way to do this was through a well-balanced but dynamic program that included academics, music, dance, drama, the arts, crafts, practical skills, cooking and nutrition, athletics, play, fun, and, always, opportunities to serve others.

As noted above, some parents saw athletic competition as detrimental to their child's well-being. They argued that setting up a situation where certain students won only when others lost went

---

95 From Master Kirpal Singh's "Humility and Simplicity," issued on July 1, 1967 (aka "The Humility Circular").
96 This was a theme Sant Ji delivered many times, including in his message to the first high school graduating class in 1978: "The earlier days of school life are like the stepping stones to the building of a person's career."

against the spirit of "Be Good. Do Good. Be One," and that competition went against non-violence. As someone who played sports in high school and college (and whose father was a coach and an athletic director) I understood that healthy competition helped build character. Like drama, art and music, athletic teams provided wonderful opportunities for children to grow. The resistance to competition was strong enough, however, that we decided to bring the question to Sant Ji.

During a visit to India in January of 1978 Karen Bicknell asked Sant Ji about the value of competition through team sports. He spoke of the positive quality of athletics, adding that he had learned games in the army. "I myself have played them," he said, "and it is very good to have them." He mentioned a number of reasons to include athletics in a school program. First, they provide exercise for the body. Next, the children benefit because they get some excitement from playing; and finally, they learn to progress and have success.

Seven years later, I reviewed with Sant Ji those early comments he shared with Karen regarding the benefits of sports. He nodded in agreement, and said, *"You can add that it increases the enthusiasm and excitement of those who see it as well as the students. It is very good for the health. It even glorifies the name of the nation!"*[97] Sant Ji was very pleased when SBS built a regulation athletic field surrounded by a 400-meter track. As he told me in 1985, "For a school it is very important to have such a ground."

---

[97] Sant Ji to me on December 4, 1984. Sant Ji himself was a champion runner as a young man and in the army. In an interview on November 30, 1988, I told Sant Ji about the successes my two sons were experiencing in the classroom and on the field. Sant Ji commented: *"And also I am very pleased to know about dear Chris and Nick's success, because you know that right from their childhood they have been with me and I always feel a lot of happiness when I hear about their success. I wish both Chris and Nick success in their lives, and I also wish that they will always be successful in their studies. And also it is very good to know that they are participating in the sports and athletics, because the time which is going to come in the near future is such that those who are participating or those who are taking part in the sports — the sportsman will be appreciated more. Because even the governments nowadays are promoting sports and appreciating and respecting the sportsmen. When I was in the army, at that time they did not used to pay so much attention to the sports. We were never encouraged and we would never get any prize if we achieved something in the sports. And what to talk about other things, we were not even given good food by the government. So nowadays they are building up this field of sports very much in India and also in all the other countries."*

85

As far as requiring students (and staff) to meditate daily, Sant Ji provided clear guidance early on when he explained to a group of teachers that it was not their role to teach students how to meditate. Instruction in the meditation process that is found in Sant Mat comes from the spiritual teacher, an adept of that practice. At the same time, it is good for children to learn the value of mindful awareness and reflection.[98] From the opening day through the present, times for sitting quietly are integrated into the daily curriculum.

Traveling the Middle Way

The fourth year seemed to fly by. Students and their families were more engaged than ever and as plans were finalized for Sant Ji's visit to Sant Bani Ashram in the spring a palpable excitement hummed throughout the campus. He was to come for the whole month of May, and after visiting various spots around the country during June and July, return to Sant Bani Ashram for three weeks in August before heading back to Rajasthan. Most teachers (and some students) had had an opportunity to visit Sant Ji at his home in India over the school year and, given the close ties of the school with Sant Mat, almost all of the non-Satsangi students and parents were looking forward to meeting him during his extended visit. Lessons in French, Spanish, history, algebra, language arts, science, math, social studies, along with art blocks, recess and clubs, continued throughout Sant Ji's residency in May.

Sant Ji requested that I come to India and help with the travel arrangements for his translator, his chanter[99] and him, which I did. We left New Delhi for America on April 26 and arrived in Boston the next day, April 27, 1977. While a full account of Sant Ji's time at Sant Bani may be found in *Rainbow On My Heart*[100] here is an excerpt covering his visit to SBS where he saw classes in session and then gave an address to the entire school community.

---

[98] See Sant Ajaib Singh, Q&A on December 12, 1976, published in *The Light of Ajaib*, Vol I, pp. 49-50.

[99] Sant Ji's public discourses generally followed an ancient template: a singer (*Pathi*) would chant verses from sacred scripture and Sant Ji would comment on them in between until the full hymn was complete.

[100] *ROMH*. See Chapters IV-VI (pp.117-211).

Sant Ji's Visit to the School on May 11, 1977

On Wednesday the 11th of May, Sant Ji came to visit the School. He walked through the original Stone Building and the addition added in 1975. He visited every class. In one, pausing at a globe, he spoke about the need to have someone who has already traveled to a country in order to understand what the country is like — that books and maps are not enough. In the same way we should have some adept of the spiritual planes to guide us within.[101]

Students, staff, and a few parents assembled in the space reserved for our daily Morning Session (the community gathering that begins each day), and the children sang some devotional songs for Sant Ji.[102] Seated on a wooden bench, Sant Ji commented that when I had gone to see him in Rajasthan a year ago, the first thing I had requested was that he visit the School. By the Grace of Master Kirpal, it was happening. He added that he was very happy to be there. His talk, captured on tape, was sweet, funny, and powerful. Sant Ji said:

The building of our life is starting, and childhood is the center stone for the foundation of the life of man. If we are wholeheartedly studying the studies which we are being taught here, and if we make our life pure, that will help us very much in our future because when we go up for further studies, the effect of this time will be on our hearts. That will not allow any bad thoughts to come in us, and that will prove very good for us, to make our future. We can get the qualities of our teachers if we respect and obey them; because if a student is obeying and respecting his teacher, the teacher gives that student much of his attention, and he helps him, and he loves him very much. That proves very good for his studies. We are studying for our own selves, and that's why we should not be angry or displeased with our teachers.

In future you will realize how much these teachings would have been helpful if you had obeyed them. Master Sawan Singh Ji used to tell about his childhood — when he was studying in school. He was living in a village named Mehmah Singh Wala, and he was going to Nanangwal, another place, for study. And when he was going there to study, first of all he would go to the teachers' home and clean the house and wash the vessels, and in that way he was respecting and doing service to his

---

[101] Aspects of this visit were captured on 8mm film. See the film titled, "Sant Ajaib Singh 1977 Visit to Sant Bani School" on Sant Bani Ashram's website: https://santbaniashram.org/videos-of-the-master/
[102] This space has been the 3rd Grade classroom for many years.

teacher very well. Even when he was getting the Engineering education in Roorkee College he was respecting and obeying his professors very much. After getting the degree, his teachers greeted him with very much respect and said, "Now there is no difference between you and us, because you also have become like us..."

We should obey our teachers and respect them because whatever they are teaching us, that is for our own good. It is said that in Rajasthan once a man was carrying four bushels of wheat on one side of his horse, and four bushels of sand on the other side, and in that way he was carrying a lot of weight on the horse. One wise man was coming from the other side and he asked the man, "What are you carrying on the horse?" He replied that, "On one side there are four bushels of wheat, but to equalize the weight I have put four bushels of sand on the other side." So the wise man told him, "Oh fool, what have you done? You should have put two bushels of wheat on either side. Why are you carrying the dust here?" But instead of accepting the wise man's advice, he became angry with him. We should not do that, because whatever wise people — whatever teachers — are telling us, that is for our own welfare...

In our days in India there weren't any very good arrangements of school and education, but then also we were three who were sent to school. One was the son of a weaver from the village, and two of us were farmer's sons. So when we went to school, our teacher gave us some lessons to learn, and then he went away for some other work. So out of the other two boys only one joined me, and we both learned that lesson very well. But the other one, he sat on the wall of the school, and he was enjoying the cool breeze coming from the other side. So when the teacher came back, he asked whether we had learned our lesson or not. We both had learned that, so he was very much pleased with us. But the other one, he said. "No. I was enjoying the cool breeze while sitting on the wall. It's very good to sit there. Why should I learn the lesson? If I want to learn the lesson, I will learn by my own self. Why are you worried about me?" I have seen him when he was grown up, and he was suffering a lot, and repenting that he hadn't obeyed his teacher.

In America it is not the usual thing to give punishment to the children, but in India it is exactly the opposite. Children are given a very good beating if they are not obeying the teacher. So when that son of the weaver didn't obey the teacher, and he didn't learn the lesson, the teacher gave him punishment. He told him, "You catch your ears." (In India, to catch one's own ears is a sign of repentance.) And when he told him to do that, instead of catching his own ears, he came to the teacher and caught the ears of the teacher. So that poor teacher was very much upset, and at last he told him to leave the school, and in that way he was thrown out from the school.

So with love we should study wholeheartedly, and we should re-
spect our teachers, because whatever they are teaching us, that is for our
good, and if we will obey them, it will make our future bright.

After the talk Sant Ji asked Pathi Ji to sing a *bhajan,* and then
he took his leave of the group. Sant Ji, Pathi Ji, Pappu, Russell,
Karen (with Nick on her back) and I walked out via the small office, and he pointed to the chair at the desk and asked me if I did
not get upset when someone else was sitting in my chair. I
laughed, and said that I did not really use that office much. Sant
Ji said, "Well, you know what I mean." He explained to us that it
is human nature to become upset when someone else seems to be
doing the work or *seva* that has been given to us. He went on to
say that the service of the Sant Bani School, the education of the
children, was very important. We needed to make the School
good.[103]

Russell, Pappu, Sant Ji, Pathi Ji, Kent, Karen and Nick

While Sant Ji visited New Hampshire several more times over
the next twenty years,[104] this first visit was the only time he stayed

---

[103] *ROMH,* pp. 135-138.
[104] Sant Ji subsequently spent time at Sant Bani Ashram in 1980, 1984, 1990 and
1996. He visited other countries at different times, and throughout his mission
(1976-1997) groups of Western disciples traveled to India to spend time with him.

at the ashram for weeks on end. As we went about the "business" of running a school for 45 elementary and high school students we recognized that having Sant Ji in our lives each day for the last five weeks of the school year was enormously helpful, hopeful and healthy. It was a unique time where we all were schooled in lessons of living in the world while nurturing the spirit. As the budding SBS emerged from its fourth year it felt like now we had graduated, and that we were, indeed, a real school poised to do great things within our walls and beyond.

Chapter V: The Fifth Year (1977-78)
A Strong Foundation

The summer of 1977 flew by as many of us were involved with Sant Ji while he toured the country in June and July. He and his party arrived back at the ashram to spend the first three weeks of August and then returned to India.[105] The school staff focused on opening for the fifth year as by now over 50 students were enrolled, including four in the 12th grade.

Students and teachers on a visiting fire truck

Jon Engle joined us as a full-time teacher whose 4th grade class became legendary. Other than a few years on Martha's Vineyard helping to found and direct a similar school, Jon spent his professional life at SBS as a beloved teacher, mentor, coach, trustee and colleague in a career that spanned several decades.

Anticipating that the schedule would be fuller than ever, we added still more full-time and part-time faculty. Shipp Webb came on board to teach elementary and secondary level classes full-time, while Tim Stamnitz offered advanced high school science courses. Mary Swan, parent, volunteered to teach first year Spanish. High

---

[105] Again, see *ROMH*, Chapter VI, "Return to New Hampshire," p.201 ff.

school level courses for 1977-78 included Algebra I and II, Geometry, Pre-Calculus, Earth Science, Biology, Astronomy, Physics, World History II, American History, French III, Spanish I, II and IV, English I, II and a combined English III-IV.

As we were now offering high school biology we wondered about dissecting specimens in class. While most of us had gone through the experience in high school or college, none of us thought it was of enough value to justify killing so many small creatures. I brought the question to Sant Ji and he supported the use of plastic models instead. He added that in his experience the students in India had grown to dislike it immensely, and he projected that the same would happen in America. It is interesting to note that just a few years ago the New Hampshire Department of Education adopted a policy that allowed students to easily opt out of any activity that involves harming animals, noting that for learning to be effective, students should "have a voice in directing their own learning pathways."[106]

To accommodate the many high school offerings, we divided the Stone Building into six tiny spaces where classes of one to four students met simultaneously. Despite the alteration in classroom design the sense of "school community" was as vibrant as ever. It was a joy to watch high school students, when not in their classroom "cubicles," interacting with children of all grade levels. SBS continued to be a fun place to learn and to teach.

When the four seniors began the process of applying to colleges and universities, the reality of preparing students for life beyond SBS struck home. While we all thought the high school offerings were solid academically, everything was so new that it was important to seek outside validation for the program. I invited two educational experts to spend the day assessing strengths and weaknesses of the curriculum. The first was Charles Marston, Assistant Division Chief of the New Hampshire Department of Education. Charlie, an enlightened educator who went on to become the New Hampshire Commissioner of Education, was at that time the primary contact person for independent schools in the state. The sec-

---

[106] See https://www.education.nh.gov/instruction/curriculum/science/student_choice.htm.

ond was Professor Thomas Johnson, an international expert in curriculum design who was the Director of the Educational Research Laboratory at the Boston University School of Education.

Both Assistant Division Chief Marston and Professor Johnson offered written critiques of the program, and together their observations provide a vivid snapshot of SBS in the early days.

Charlie Marston's Letter of Evaluation

November 17, 1977

Dear Mr. Bicknell:

I wish to thank you, the students, and members of your staff for the informative and interesting day spent visiting Sant Bani Ashram School on October 27, 1977. The rural setting in one of the most beautiful areas of our state enhances the "sense of community" that one feels in attempting to describe the unique features of the school environment.

I was particularly impressed with the natural and caring relationships exhibited between the younger and older children. The genuine interest and helping attitude expressed by the high school students for their younger counterparts reflect their sense of responsibility and service to others which is so much a part of Sant Bani Ashram's religious and educational mission.

In assessing the secondary school program, I am of the opinion that the offerings in language arts, foreign languages, the social studies, sciences, mathematics, and the fine arts provide the nucleus for a sound preparation in the academic disciplines and basic skills areas. The current efforts to expand the number of student activities, including athletics, together with the staff commitment to evaluation demonstrate a professional concern to meet the increasingly diverse needs of a growing enrollment.

My initial impression of the school's instructional climate is that it provides for sufficient structure, but without the rigidity that so often stifles the individual student's needs for self-expression. In this sense, I was pleased to observe the orderly, organized classroom environment and the general enthusiasm displayed by the students for their studies. The highly personalized approach to instruction is enhanced by small classes and the obvious sense of "worth" in which each student is held by the staff. Students with whom I talked demonstrated those qualities of self-assurance and self-discipline that only "trusting" relationships can nurture. This observation speaks well of the professional training and general competence of administrative and teaching personnel. In fact, the quality of the human relationships is truly one of the distinguishing characteristics of Sant Bani Ashram School.

Thank you for the opportunity to visit your school and every best wish for continued growth and success.

Sincerely yours,
Charles H. Marston
Assistant Division Chief
New Hampshire Department of Education

Thomas Johnson's Letter of Evaluation

December 20, 1977

Dear Kent:

Thank you for inviting me to visit the Sant Bani Ashram School. During my visit, I talked to students, and observed the quality of instruction briefly at the elementary level, and in four separate classes at the high school level. These included English III, Physics, Algebra II, and Astronomy. I want to take this opportunity to share with you my evaluation of the status of the educational program at the high school level.

While the format of the classes would be expected to vary somewhat across the content covered, they all demonstrated the manner in which an informal, relaxed classroom instructional setting can be used to pursue the acquisition of a well-structured body of knowledge. By way of example, the English class had been studying the Dickens novel, *Tale of Two Cities*, for the week immediately preceding my visit. As an English major, and a former high school English teacher, I had some normative basis for judging that the instructor asked penetrating, sophisticated questions about main characters, story plot, etc. — questions that were more appropriate at the college level. Thus, initially I was quite surprised at the uniform high quality of student responses to these questions. When I talked to several students after the class some of the reasons underlying the superior performances became clear. A large part of performances is attributable to the systematic analytic techniques and note-taking ("scholarly inquiry?") that the instructor has taught, and which is required of each student as they read through the novels, and other literature

94

covered by the course. It is an excellent instructional technique, one that supports active class participation in discussion, and assures a fairly uniform high quality of learning.

The Physics class I observed was dealing with the mechanics of motion organized around problem sets. The informal instructional style was again present. There were fairly open discussions either about how to conceptualize the problems for their solution, or why certain solutions would or would not work. High school physics at this level is a course that combines logic with mathematics. The level of mathematics competency obviously varied among the students, which normally would lead to an uneven quality of participation across the problem sets. The instructor was especially good at restating problems to focus on the logical forms when the students were confused about mathematical forms. This procedure seemed to permit most students to participate effectively, and to cover the same content at about the same rate. This procedure also is an excellent way to accommodate a general mix of student types in the class.

The instructional format of the Astronomy and Algebra classes was consistent with the English and Physics, and the quality of student participation was high in both these classes as well.

I did not have any knowledge about the planned relationship between the elementary and high school curriculum to react to the sense in which your educational program has a cumulative effect on the students.

I was impressed with several distinguishing features of the students I observed. Without exception, they were busy at being students. They study the material, were prepared, were focused, and seemed to enjoy the intellectual challenge of the content area. Maybe this was all part of a "put on" for the outside observer, but it would be hard to maintain such a role over all classes. I'm convinced it is a real phenomenon but don't know if it is a planned part of the program or how it is done. That kind of attitude and performance in the role of student is one that I don't often see. It is refreshing to see whenever it occurs and I hope you will continue to foster it as a formal part of your program.

Best wishes,
Thomas J. Johnson, Director
Educational Research Laboratory,
Boston University School of Education

It was uplifting to receive this feedback from two professionals who had a wealth of experience with different kinds of schools. With their permission, we included copies of these letters in the application material prepared for various colleges and universities.

Along with a need to validate our program, we wondered what the social transition would be like for our students. A number of adults were of the opinion that we were "sheltering students from reality," and we also had questions about how the "culture shock" of university life might impact our 12th graders. I recall lengthy discussions with Mildred and Russell where we tried to imagine changing our "reality" to conform more with conventional practices. We kept coming back to the value of what we were doing as recently acknowledged by two outside experts — of educating the whole child in a loving, supportive and joyful environment where we all learned from each other — and concluded that we did not wish to alter our approach. At the same time, we understood the validity of concerns around transition to college and chose to seek counsel from Sant Ji.

Preparing Students for Life Beyond SBS:
Excerpt from *Rainbow On My Heart*

I was very busy — teaching full time at the school as well as directing it, and traveling to Boston each week to complete my doctoral courses, as instructed by Sant Ji. He often asked about my progress toward the degree, reminding me that both He and Hazur Kirpal would be pleased when I had reached that goal. Several times He wrote that He would be very happy when the day came that He could call me, "Doctor Kent Bicknell, Principal Sahib!" As I was able to include a second level Hindi course as part of my studies, I eagerly wrote to Sant Ji as often as I could — and He always wrote back. If a subject were complicated, subtle, or the answer critical to others, however, I wrote in English.

Guidance for Sant Bani School

We had initially intended the school to serve through grade eight only. Responding to community needs, we began to accept high school students in our third year (1975-1976). By the fall of 1977, we had four seniors — and we naturally had concerns about how they would fare beyond the rather protected walls of Sant

96

Bani. A second question came from some parents who wished that we had less emphasis on academics, and more on vocational skills. We wondered if it would be appropriate to begin more practical training for students — to accompany the academic program. With these thoughts in mind, I wrote to Sant Ji on December 8, 1977.

I have two questions about the school that I want to ask you. Karen will be coming next month and will bring a couple of other questions about the school at that time.

The first is about the high school. At present we are preparing the students to go on to college and encouraging the ones that can go to college to do so. Some people, however, feel that college is a waste of time and money, and that we should be preparing the students by training them in practical skills so they can get a job in the world. We will do both someday, but at present we are emphasizing the preparation for college through school studies of mathematics, science, history, etc. Is this in accordance with your wishes?

Also, sometimes we worry about the students when they will be going off to college. Here they have a very protecting environment, and are supported by the ashram. But in college they will be surrounded by people involved in worldly pursuits, pleasures, etc. Some of the students and teachers worry that it will be hard for them to be strong on the Path and also to make new friends, etc. What can the school do to help prepare the high school students for going out in the world, especially to college?

On December 17, 1977, Sant Ji responded as follows:

Both the types of studies are good at their own places. I am pleased with that. But as you mentioned in the letter about giving practical training to students and preparing them for jobs, I will be much pleased if some day by Hazur's grace you will start giving them such training in your school.

You should not worry about the future of students because every body has his own karmas, his own fate. As long as they are under your guidance you should do your best. If the foundation of a building is strong, that building won't fall down easily. In the same way, if your studies and teachings will have much impression on them, they won't get spoiled easily. If a student, who has got good education in his childhood, goes in bad company, he will realize his mistake very soon. So please don't be worried for student's future. Do your best.[107]

---

[107] *ROMH*, pp. 213-215.

We took Sant Ji's advice to heart and over the years made significant progress in providing practical training to students. The annual Projects Period (see below) has often included "shadowing" a professional. Enrichment blocks, clubs and service projects are frequently grounded in real-world practical experiences. At the same time we were encouraged by Sant Ji's sage counsel regarding the experiences of our graduates. Obviously there was no way we could (or would wish to) control what happened to our students after they left; on the other hand Sant Ji made it clear that grounding students in good teachings would help them adjust and realize any inevitable "mistakes" they made sooner. Our role was to "do our best" to help them build a strong foundation.

Interest in SBS continued to grow as more families in the area heard about the school and Satsangi families from around the country moved to the area. To help with math we hired Jonathan Powell, a recent Dartmouth graduate and Satsangi who was working as an upholsterer, to work part-time. Jonathan went on to devote his professional life to building the quality of the program while serving as teacher, mentor, tutor, administrator and business manager for almost four decades.

Mid-year we needed another math teacher and I wished to hire a current parent who I thought would be excellent. Up until this point the only teachers at SBS were Satsangis, and as this parent was not a follower of Sant Mat, concerns were raised. I understood from my conversations with Miss Sati at Master Kirpal's school in India that being a Satsang was not a prerequisite; after all, Master Kirpal had advised her to put an ad in the local paper and hire the most qualified teachers that applied.[108] For everyone's peace of mind, however, I decided it was best to bring the matter directly to Sant Ji.

I explained the situation to him in detail. The school needed a good math teacher; this parent was excellent; she understood the school and its values very well as her children were here — but some were objecting because she was not a Satsangi. Sant Ji was quiet for a time and then asked me, "Will this parent eat meat on the campus?" When I made it clear she would not, he responded, "Well

---

[108] See Chapter I: "Winter Interlude: Six Weeks in India"

then what is the problem?" adding that it would be fine to hire her. We did, and she taught at SBS for decades.

The media continued to be interested in what we were doing, and articles like the following two were instrumental in spreading the word about SBS and its unique approach throughout central New Hampshire.

Outside Perspectives

Ashram School Growing[109]
by John N. Buckland

All except the state's most handsomely endowed private schools are feeling the crunch caused by skyrocketing costs, a depressed economy, and most recently, a kick in the academic derrière by the Supreme Court in disallowing use of public money in the operations of non-public schools... The Sant Bani Ashram School, however, appears to be faring considerably better than its counterparts nationwide. The reason being that the school is not just financially backed but is spiritually backed and is motivated by the purpose that it is serving... The spiritual aspect of the school emphasizes the importance of certain fundamental ideas found in many of the world's religions and the lives of great men and women: the equality of humans under God; a reverence of life in all its forms; a dedication to serving others...

An important part of the curriculum centers on the concept of service. Students do much of the maintenance of the school, including tending the wood stoves, bringing in wood and cleaning... Most of this is done on a volunteer basis during free time, in keeping with the principle that the highest service is selfless service, not a forced service...

The secondary school day is divided into six periods, and students have five classes and one study hall daily. The academic approach is "traditional" in that the school curriculum consists primarily of typical high school level courses. Graduation requirements include four years of English; three years each of mathematics, history, foreign languages and science; and a typing course. The average time students spend on homework is three

---

[109] The copy of this article, unfortunately has neither a date nor a header to show where/when it was published. It is clear from the content that the journalist visited sometime in the 1977-78 academic year.

hours daily. Basic academic skills are taught at the lower level and reinforced, where necessary, at the upper level.

The size of the school promotes certain activities and limits others. Concepts such as class rank or class officers are irrelevant, and interscholastic athletics are not possible. The mix of grades 1-12 allows for considerable vertical grouping, and interaction between younger and older children is a way of life for the school. Ages of the participants of any given game are likely to span 60 years (including staff)! Sportsman-like conduct and the value of team play are emphasized. High school students have the opportunity for involvement in activities such as ceramics, weaving, stained glass, linoleum block prints, drama and music.

Some are skeptical of the concepts practiced by the Sant Bani School. The best proof is to visit the school and observe the children learning. And to be convinced that there is more to an education than the academic aspects. That children need to be taught not only academically but mentally, socially, spiritually, and emotionally.

"Education is a vital force in the life of any child," said Kent Bicknell, principal of the Sant Bani School. "Even in its traditional sense of that which occurs in school, its potential for influencing children, either positively or negatively, is very great, as well as quite real."

The next piece, published in late May, featured a photo of the four seniors, captioned, "*FIRST GRADUATING CLASS at the Sant Bani Ashram School consists of Stephen Rucker, Melissa Powers, Evelyn Sanborn and Carolyn Hammond, with graduation set for June 9. The four have been accepted at a variety of colleges.*"

Ashram School Mushrooms in Sanbornton
by Edith L. Costa
The New Hampshire Sunday News, May 28, 1978

SANBORNTON, May 27 – As the first graduating class of the Sant Bani Ashram School prepares for commencement June 9, Principal Kent Bicknell now anticipates plans for extensive expansion of the school which began only five years ago with six students.

"We had no idea the school would grow so fast," Bicknell said, still amazed that enrollment has doubled each year since 1973. The first addition, a library and two classrooms, was necessary after only two years of operation.

"When we started with grades 1-8 we were not sure we would ever get into high school education," Bicknell noted. "We anticipated expansion to maybe 25 students, and thought that would take several years. All along we have had to respond to demand. We have never advertised locally, never publicized the school. Yet by the nature of the community and surrounding communities, we have become more widely known."

"As the high school program expanded, we had to offer so many more courses and improvise with walls placed in the library to establish adequate classrooms. The 10 high school students are offered 17 to 18 courses."

OPEN TO ALL

The Sant Bani Ashram School is situated on 200 acres of woods and fields in central New Hampshire, a day school with 60 students in grades 1-12. The school is an outgrowth of the Sant Bani Ashram, a religious retreat dedicated to awareness of God and humankind through meditation and service.

The educational program is open to all, regardless of religion, race, sex, or economic status, with the basic tuition fees set according to actual cost per student, the fees low and flexible.

Participation in the rigorous way of life adopted by ashram residents and guests is not a requirement for students in the school.

The school is fully accredited by the New Hampshire State Department of Education. While still too small to apply for accreditation by the New England Association of Schools and Colleges,[110] its four graduates this year have been accepted at a wide variety of schools. Carolyn Hammond has been accepted at Vassar, Evelyn Sanborn at Colby Sawyer College. Melissa Powers has been accepted at Alfred, Franklin Pierce, and New England College and plans to attend the New England College branch in England. Stephen Rucker has been accepted at Plymouth and Keene State colleges.

Instructors at the school could probably earn at least twice as much in other situations, Bicknell noted. None of them make more than $7000 a year. Mary Swan, who teaches Spanish I, has two children in the school. She donates this course. Many others do the same. Some teachers take their meals at the ashram as part of their salary.

---

[110] Since 1992 Sant Bani School has been accredited by the NEASC.

"We never have much money in the bank," the young principal said, with a laugh, "but expenses are covered by tuition and donations, with donations covering up to 40-50% of costs."

Such things as salaries and educational materials are covered by tuitions, set at $1100. If all parents paid this amount, it would be fine, but many can't pay the full tuition and some cannot pay any.

"We work it out with what the family can realistically pay," Bicknell said. "The school was founded on the premise that no child should be denied admission on the basis of financial hardship. This makes us heavily dependent on donations. Each year they have come through extremely well and without any fund-raising program."

It may be a little more difficult to meet costs of the proposed new triangular addition, though Boston architect Victor Jorrin is donating his services. This construction, estimated to cost several hundred thousand dollars, will incorporate a passive solar heating system.[111]

Students volunteer for much of the maintenance of the school. Students also have been involved in building the school, working in the vegetable gardens, planting flowers, and cooking and serving meals to guests.

In a talk in 1972 the school's founder, Kirpal Singh, said, "In fact, the real aim of education is to develop the character and individuality of the pupil, his mind, will and soul power. The best education is that which teaches us that the end of knowledge is service." Service, he explained, is another name for love and fellowship, which constitute the very essence of personal and social life.

He also said, "It is the proper atmosphere which can deliver the goods. That is why emphasis in the school should be on atmosphere more than on rules, textbooks, and buildings."

As experienced at the ashram school, the theory not only is pleasant to observe — it seems to work.

---

[111] This construction did not happen as SBS acquired neighboring properties to address the growth of the campus.

The Birth of Clubs and Projects Period

Two long-established features of SBS began at this time: Clubs and Projects Period. Setting aside a special time for afternoon Clubs on Friday was a response to a need expressed by a parent who lived a good distance from the campus. At a general parent meeting she observed that her children got home too late to participate in after-school activities such as the local chapter of Brownies, and wondered if the school could offer similar options. Acknowledging this need, the faculty developed Friday afternoon Clubs with an array of choices off-campus and on, including skiing, skating, snowshoeing, swimming, horseback riding, tennis, service, mountain biking, hiking and many other exciting opportunities our students might otherwise have missed.

As noted in Chapter III, Robert Schongalla came to Sant Bani after teaching at nearby New Hampton School. We all were intrigued when he shared that New Hampton created time for small groups of students and faculty to experience something not available on campus. Calling it "Projects Period," the program allowed an individualized off-campus learning experience that was student-designed and then implemented over a period of one to two weeks. This approach harmonized well with our commitment to project-based learning and we were eager to implement something similar. The timing coincided with the development of the ashram arranging monthly trips to India for Satsangis to spend ten days in a meditation retreat with Sant Ajaib Singh. We wondered about the idea of creating a "Teachers Group" from SBS that would travel to India while students were involved off-campus in completing individual projects of their own design. We tried it, and it worked quite well.

While groups of teachers from SBS no longer head to India in February/March (and have not for decades) the potential of Projects Period continues to be realized as SBS students propose and complete an array of exceptional projects year after year. As noted on the School's website, *"Projects Period encourages each child to take risks, and builds confidence to explore individual interests, try out new roles, follow their curiosity and be creative. At the end of the break, two days of school time are set aside for sharing. Each student describes his or her project, and students and teachers take turns serving on teams to evaluate the project and the quality of presentation. These evaluations are shared with the student. All projects are displayed on the Wednesday evening following our return from break."* [112]

Finishing Year Five in Style:
L. Frank Baum's *The Wonderful Wizard of Oz*

During the late spring the whole school became involved in a production of L. Frank Baum's *The Wizard of Oz*. As Helen Perkins described above, Russell adapted the book and the movie (both of which he almost knew by heart) to create a full-blown musical directed by Mildred that included intricate choreography, a live band, elaborate costumes and make-up, and lots of practice time. Students, staff and volunteers skillfully filled the adventures of Dorothy and her companions with an abundance of energy, joy and stagecraft as the musical was performed superbly on a stage that included sophisticated props such as a trap-door (to accommodate a "melting" witch) and a flying air-balloon. The students in grades 1-12 brought the fantastical land of Oz to life for both the audience and themselves.

Russell's perspective on *The Wizard of Oz* was that it was a spiritual allegory about the soul's search to find its source, its True Home, and the journey back to it. The extensive program notes laid out this esoteric interpretation of Oz for all.

Program Notes: *The Wizard of Oz*

The Wonderful Wizard of Oz, as it was then titled, first appeared as a children's book in 1900. It told the now-familiar story of the (presumably) orphaned Kansas farm-girl Dorothy, blown in her house by a cyclone to a marvelous fairyland ruled over by a mysterious Wizard who never reveals his true form. Dorothy's efforts to get home (beginning with her arrival encased in her house) bring about tremendous changes both in the fairyland itself and in the lives of individuals she meets, so that by the time she was sent home the fairyland's future is altered irrevocably. Nevertheless her main interest is, always and in everything, in going home, and she is finally sent home — by the one person in the

---

[112] See http://www.santbani.org/program/projects_period/

fairyland who has the ability to show her how to make use of that which she already has.

Reduced to its essentials, it is obvious that the story is a parable of the home-going of the soul; yet it is possible that no story in our literature has been less understood or more underrated. Only recently has *The Wizard of Oz* begun to be taken seriously by academic critics; for years it was considered "just a story" to be enjoyed only, unlike other children's stories which were loaded with meaning. Even today many people who earn their living through children's literature perpetuate this myth. But it isn't true (although, of course, it is intensely enjoyable).

The thing to be grasped immediately is the respective positions of Oz and Kansas. Most people with some knowledge of spiritual ideas assume that the land of Oz is "the inner planes" or the other world, and dreary gray Kansas is the physical plane — this world. This is exactly wrong. Kansas is dreary and gray only to eyes which have not yet understood the value of fulfillment and peace, and are addicted to color and excitement. It is dreary because nothing "happens" there; but that also makes it peaceful to those who have learned the transitory nature of excitement. The land of Oz, "where the action is," is filled with color and adventure which, like the world we live in, quickly becomes a nightmare; and Dorothy's experiences there consist, basically, of one disappointment after another, sweetened with a little bit of love and humor between the heartbreaks.

Dorothy cannot appreciate Kansas because she has not developed those aspects of herself which can discriminate between true values and false ones. The only way she can find out is to experience the false ones personally; so the cyclone carries her away from action-less Kansas to the "*Dharam Khand*" or Realm of Action — the land of Oz, where things *happen*! It does not take Dorothy long — about five minutes — to realize that regardless of the color and drama of Oz, Kansas is where she wants to be; and she maintains that for the rest of the story.

By virtue of her arrival in Oz — not because of anything she has consciously or willfully done — she earns the right to the Silver Shoes, which eventually take her home; just as by virtue of our human birth — and not because of anything we can remember doing — we earn the birthright to go back to our Real Home. Soon after her arrival (and here, as in all parables, time is greatly foreshortened; the events of several lifetimes are crowded into a short period) she meets Glinda, the Good Witch, who gives her the Kiss of Protection, and later on, when she has fulfilled her destiny, shows her how to use the Silver Shoes. Glinda thus fulfills the two classic functions of a *Guru* — (1) protection, and (2) showing the disciple how to use that which he already has in order to return to the Real Home.

Negativity in Oz, just as in our world, functions in two ways: as obvious evil (in the person of the Wicked Witch) and in a much subtler form, as ultimate dishonesty (in the person of the Wizard). The Witch is by far the easiest to overcome; a real primeval nightmare figure out of the worst fears of our childhood, she cannot be stopped or suppressed by any of the usual means; but she can be melted. The Wizard (as is the case with our ego) cannot be overcome at all; he can only be exposed. Once seen for what he really is, the only appropriate action is to stop counting on him. If what we ask of him is still within his realm, (as with Dorothy's companions) and is illusory to begin with, then he can satisfy us; but any attempt to rely on him to take us Home — that is, from illusion to reality — is doomed to defeat, because his wizard-ness is of the nature of illusion. It is interesting to note the progression by which Dorothy is led on, step by step: Glinda sends her to the Wizard; the Wizard demands that she destroy the Witch; once this is done, the exposure of the Wizard follows of necessity, because his Wizard-self cannot handle the reality of the new situation.

Also important are the changes that take place in the land of Oz externally as the result of Dorothy's successful quest. The two Wicked Witches are dead and the false Wizard, who had no right to rule the land, has left; while the Scarecrow is left in charge, he has no right to rule either, and in the second Oz book, *The Marvelous Land of Oz* (1904), he and the Tin Woodman help Glinda discover where the rightful ruler — Princess Ozma — is and restore her to the throne. With the return of Ozma, the land of Oz leaves the Dark Age (*Kali Yuga*) of the first book and enters into its Golden Age. In the third book (*Ozma of Oz*, 1907) Dorothy returns, becomes friendly with Ozma, and helps her exorcise a new evil figure (the Nome King) not in Oz, this time, but just across its borders. In the fourth book, *Dorothy and the Wizard in Oz* (1908) the Wizard returns, purified by *his* return home, sits at Glinda's feet and eventually becomes a real Wizard. Ultimately Dorothy herself settles in Oz permanently as a Princess, and brings Uncle Henry and Aunt Em with her to live in what is now a Utopia far removed indeed from the "uncivilized" land of the first story. By this time the original significance of Oz in relation to Kansas has shifted drastically, but this is directly due to Dorothy's intervention in Oz affairs and her personal success. Oz's Golden Age came about because of what Dorothy did in her efforts to return Home.

****

L. Frank Baum, the creator of the Oz mythos and the author of the story from which this play is adapted, and who appears in our version as the Teller of the Tale, is one of the most interesting figures in American literary history. His original aspiration was to be a playwright, and he did have one success, *The Maid of Arran*, in the 1880s; but all of his other plays failed and he held a variety of other jobs — e.g., manager of a general store, editor of a small weekly newspaper — and was generally (by himself, perhaps, as well as others) considered a failure. He was happily married (and remained so all of his life) to Maud Gage, daughter of Matilda Joslyn Gage, one of the leading feminists of the day; she never lost faith in him, and he, long before Wonder Woman, filled the Oz books with a galaxy of female characters surely unrivaled anywhere. In *The Wizard of Oz*, for example, all the strong characters — Dorothy, the heroine, the accomplisher; Glinda, the Guru-figure, the personification of good; the Wicked Witch, the personification of evil; and Aunt Em, the God-figure — are all female. This pattern, although occasionally broken, remains the dominant one throughout the Oz series.

In 1899, he published *Father Goose: His Book*, a collection of children's poems which was moderately successful. The following year came *The Wizard of Oz*, an instant and lasting success which established Baum's popular reputation as a children's writer. Although he was a middle-aged man by this time, he went on to write more than sixty books for children, many of them under pseudonyms. His fourteen Oz books were then and are now by far the most popular. They have been in print continuously since their publication, and are in print to this day.

As for Baum's personal philosophy, the following quotes from *The Annotated Wizard of Oz*, by Michael Patrick Hearn (pp. 69, 72-73) are illuminating: "The author of *The Wizard of Oz* was indeed well read in the occult sciences. When he lived in Aberdeen [South Dakota], Baum became interested in Theosophy and was rumored to be a Buddhist... He firmly believed in reincarnation; he had faith in the immortality of the soul... He was in agreement with the Theosophist belief that man on earth was only one step on a great ladder that passed through many states of consciousness, through many universes, to a final state of Enlightenment. He did believe in Karma, that whatever good or evil one does in his lifetime returns to him as reward or punishment in future reincarnations... He believed that all the great religious teachers of history had found their inspiration from the same source, a common Creator. He would not accept the rivalries between different sects."

When asked how he came to write the first Oz book, he said, "It was pure inspiration. It came to me right out of the blue. I think that sometimes the Great Author has a message to get across and He has to use the instrument at hand..."

He died in 1919 — a great American author in the tradition of Emerson, Thoreau and Whitman. This version of his story is dedicated to his memory.

Russell Perkins

Successfully staging this musical — homegrown in so many ways — was a "wonderful" way to wind up the school year. The multi-age production set a very high standard for drama at SBS that students and staff continue to meet. The four 12th graders, the Wizard/Storyteller (Stephen), Aunt Em (Carolyn), the Wicked Witch of the West (Evelyn) and Private Omby Amby (Melissa) were so dedicated to getting the production right that they were willing to have the play performed two weeks after they graduated![113]

First High School Graduation

We were excited to be holding our first-ever high school graduation in early June, as the seniors were ready for life beyond SBS. We planned a simple ceremony, using the pond down near the Master's House as a backdrop. As we talked about the features we wanted to see in an SBS graduation, of primary importance was that each graduate had a chance to say something. We wondered whether it made sense to have an outside speaker who did not really know the school, and decided that students should choose someone from the staff to share words of wisdom. All along we wanted to ask Sant Ji if he would provide a message, which he graciously agreed to do. To engage the whole community we decided to close with a favorite hymn that had been sung often over the

---

[113] Our newly minted alumni also rallied to help build and populate (in costumes and make up) the school's Oz-based float, "There's No Place Like Home," that won top prize in Sanbornton's Old Home Day Parade that summer.

years, "Amazing Grace." Once the "official" ceremony was complete we would head up to the Stone/Wooden Building for a reception.

The first high school graduation ceremony

Friday June 9th was a beautiful early summer day for seniors, students, faculty, family and friends to gather at the pond. We opened with recorder music played by students, followed by an invocation from faculty spouse Reverend David Teed. I welcomed everyone and then read Sant Ji's message:[114]

Dear Children,
On this occasion I send my congratulations to all the students who are going to step into the world after completing their high school studies.
The earlier days of school life are like the stepping stone to the building of man's career. You will be meeting many people in the world; will see many things in the world. Many ups and downs might come, but always remember your goal, which you have to accomplish.
The most important thing which every student must do is to respect the teacher and keep himself devoted to studies with full

---

[114] *ROMH*, p. 264.

concentration. Our teacher or professor is a mine of knowledge. If we will respect him, he will give us the riches of knowledge, for which we go to college.

I pray to Almighty God to guide you and bless you with wisdom and right understanding in every aspect of life. My love and best wishes are always with all of you.

With all His love,

Ajaib Singh

I called each graduate to receive her/his diploma, and then Carolyn, Melissa, Stephen and Evelyn were invited to share their thoughts. Russell offered some closing remarks, and after a benediction we all sang "Amazing Grace." With much laughter and a few tears we congratulated the new alumni and headed for the delicious treats that awaited. The simple, elegant and beautiful ceremony set the stage for graduations to come.

For the next two weeks we madly rehearsed *The Wizard of Oz*. It was presented to the public on three successive nights starting Thursday, June 22, and as the curtain fell on the final production, we closed Year Five.

The first-prize-winning Oz float at Sanbornton's Old Home Day parade

Chapter VI: The Unending Process of Learning

Life is an unending process of learning.
Sant Ajaib Singh to the SBS Class of 1992

Reflections

The epigraph of Sant Ajaib Singh on the title page of this book — *The earlier days of school life are like the stepping stones to the building of a person's career* — is as true for the school as it is for individuals. The first five years of Sant Bani School laid the foundation not only for the four decades that came after but also for today and tomorrow. At the same time, as Sant Ji notes above, life really is an unending process of learning, and everyone involved with the school has continued to learn throughout the journey.

Renowned environmentalist Paul Hawken once observed that while core values are timeless, the modalities for delivering them change all the time.[115] This final chapter outlines a number of steps taken as the school evolved to meet ever-changing needs while remaining true to its mission.

A consistent theme the school has heard almost since inception is that it is "mission-driven." That SBS lives its mission stands out not only in the newspaper articles and letters from professional educators featured above, but as an overarching theme in the three accreditation visits (1992, 2002 and 2012) by a team of NEASC[116] colleagues and by visitors today. As a member of over a dozen visiting teams that spent time on campuses throughout New England, I became keenly aware that to say a school "lives its mission" is high praise in an era when educational institutions, along with many other organizations, struggle to stay true to their purpose.

---

[115] Paul Hawken in conversation with the author in July 2014, Mill Valley, CA.
[116] NEASC is the New England Association of Schools and Colleges, the accreditation organization for New England schools ranging from Sant Bani to MIT and Harvard.

The lightning pace of the 21st century has led to an identity crisis for many schools, particularly as they compete to attract students.[117]

New schools often create a mission statement before they open their doors and then work to live up to it. From the beginning SBS was fortunate to have Master Kirpal Singh's "Toward the New Education" as a guiding document. The school then added veteran educators and eager young professionals to bring this "New Education" to life. By the time the school drafted its first mission statement the community had been living it for well over a decade. This is one reason why the foundation laid in the early years is so clearly reflected in the current mission, values and core commitments/operating principles of SBS:

> **Mission**: Sant Bani School is built on the belief that we have something to learn from everyone. Surrounded by nature, we create a diverse community where respect for all living things is central. Our mission is to provide a high-level, comprehensive educational experience while also recognizing the value of the spirit. With small classes, committed faculty, and an emphasis on collaboration and service to others, Sant Bani School teaches students to Be Good, Do Good, Be One.

> **We value**:
> - an open, judgment-free environment that builds confidence and encourages curiosity and creativity
> - academic, social and emotional learning
> - collaboration and critical thinking
> - mutual respect, fairness and inclusiveness
> - service to others, connecting empathy and generosity of spirit with action
> - nature and the experience of being outdoors
> - quiet time, simplicity and reflection
> - expanding students' horizons and connecting with the world around us
> - having fun together

> **Essential Commitments | Core Operating Principles:** The following operating principles expressed by the spiritual teachers

---

[117] This rang true in the schools I evaluated/consulted with in Guatemala, India and Bhutan as well as in the material I reviewed for over 100 schools in my six years as a Commissioner with the NEASC.

H.H. Kirpal Singh (1894-1974) and Sant Ajaib Singh (1926-1997) will be sustained in perpetuity by the School.

1. Understand and appreciate that every person is unique and, as such, that there is something to learn from everyone.
2. Pursue learning with the objective of being better able to help others. The school-wide service-learning program brings this principle to life.
3. Demonstrate kindness to and respect for all living things. The practice of requiring vegetarian meals during school and at school events reflects this principle on a daily basis.[118]

In 1983 Sant Ajaib Singh emphatically endorsed the idea that Sant Bani School would outlive us all.[119] The essential purpose of the school, to educate children in a beneficial way, would continue even without a connection to a living spiritual teacher. This is possible because the fundamental role of a school is to provide a strong foundation that will allow each student to develop her/his authentic self and find success in life. As Sant Ji said after visiting the school's new playing field and classrooms in 1990, *"Worldly knowledge is equally as important as spiritual knowledge – because you need the worldly knowledge, the good education, to make your life in this world. The donors who gave to make these buildings and to support the school will get a lot of benefit because the students will gain a lot from coming here."*[120]

To provide students the knowledge on which they can "make their life" requires a program that is both current and understands the challenges of tomorrow. To that end it is important for a school to "keep making changes according to the requirement of society and the present situation of the world."[121] This is exactly what SBS has done. Delivery methods for the curriculum are up-to-date and the modalities for conveying timeless core values have been adapted to fit the times. The result is a strong institution built on the principles outlined in "Toward the New Education." Over the

---

[118] Adopted by the Sant Bani School Board of Trustees, November, 2014.
[119] In conversation with the author in India, November, 1983. See below for details.
[120] July 19, 1990.
[121] From the 1991 letter Sant Ji wrote to a school teacher in Massachusetts cited at length in Chapter IV.

years SBS has educated hundreds of students from diverse backgrounds as it continually brings to life the dream of Master Kirpal Singh and his early followers.

Challenges and Gratitude

For the first decade SBS was run as a service of Sant Bani Ashram. In 1983 Sant Ji suggested it would be best for both the ashram and the school to become separate organizations. In his initial letter about this change he wrote, *"I would like to advise you that you should start thinking about making Sant Bani Ashram School as a separate organization. This will be better in every way. We will talk more about this when you come in the next group."*[122]

A primary reason for creating separate legal entities was that the purpose of the two organizations was distinct. The ashram was to help individual seekers connect to a spiritual path and the school was for educating children. Second, the overall budget of the school was becoming so much larger than that of the ashram that it no longer made sense to operate SBS under the umbrella of the ashram. Finally, both Master Kirpal Singh and Sant Ajaib Singh stressed that there should be no efforts to seek donations on behalf of the ashram, since, like all gifts of nature, spirituality should be free. From the school's inception, however, Master Kirpal made it clear that we would need to raise funds to support operating costs. He advised us to charge fees for tuition and then ask the Sangat (the congregation) to help cover the deficit.

Sant Ji reiterated that advice often, telling me on a number of occasions that I should not hesitate to share the school's financial needs with those who could afford to assist, and they would help. He pointed out that donating was beneficial for the givers as well as the school. In 1990 he wrote to a benefactor:

> Dear Kent Bicknell has recently told me about the progress of Sant Bani School and I am most grateful for all of your efforts to help.
> It is written in the Hindu scriptures that there are six deeds which are considered as the most pious: one is to perform the austerities and the second is to make others perform; the third is to

---

[122] Letter from Sant Ajaib Singh to the author, November 3, 1983.

give the donation and the fourth is to receive; the fifth is to receive the education and the last is to make others receive the education.

Many children have received much benefit from Sant Bani School and in the future also many more will receive. To help such a cause definitely bears fruit.

The school has always relied on the generous support of friends to provide for students in need of financial aid, and the response of benefactors throughout its history has been nothing short of extraordinary. Time and again the donors have indicated their desire to give silently, with no public recognition. Each donor knows who s/he is, however, and the school remains eternally grateful for every one of these past, present and future gifts of Grace. With ongoing support SBS continues to offer assistance to families in need, ensuring that the school will remain true to the wish voiced by the spiritual teachers that the student body be inclusive rather than exclusive.

When Sant Ji wrote in 1983 to suggest that the time had come for the school and ashram to be separate entities, he added that we would talk more about this when I came to India. Two weeks after receiving the letter I traveled to India and we spoke at length about the proposed reorganization. He clarified how important it was to do this for a number of reasons, including that the school would own the land under its buildings and that our governing body could be reconstituted to include non-Satsangis as well as Satsangis. He also suggested we use the opportunity to change the name from "Sant Bani Ashram School" to "Sant Bani School," adding that *"nobody should feel badly about this. When you have a separate organization, it is appropriate to have a separate name."* [123] As the translator, Pappu, and I sat in Sant Ji's small room in India and absorbed his guidance for the future, it struck me that SBS had the potential to serve generations of children. I shared that thought aloud and Sant Ji enthusiastically agreed. Years later Pappu conveyed how Sant Ji imagined Sant Bani School would be there for ages: that the school would definitely have a purpose and life beyond the three of us who had been sitting in that room at that point in time. [124]

---

[123] Conversations with Sant Ajaib Singh in November, 1983.
[124] Conversation with Pappu in May, 2012.

The school and the ashram began the process of becoming separate non-profits and arranged for transferring ownership of the land that housed school buildings. Several individuals, non-Satsangis as well as Satsangis, were invited to join the new board of trustees.[125] Of this original group, a number served for decades, including Whit Smith (president) and Charlie Boynton (treasurer), who continue to offer leadership at the board level as of 2018.

Along with donors and trustees, there are so many others who worked hard to build and sustain SBS over the years. These include not only faculty and staff but alumni, students, parents and volunteers. At the same time that SBS has received an enormous amount of financial support through donations, parents have helped sustain the school in so many ways. This has included assisting in the classroom and on the playing field as well as seemingly endless rounds of weekend cleaning and providing other needed services, the total savings of which has never been calculated.

Perhaps none have given as much as the faculty and staff, past and present, who have worked so hard to offer a first-class education at SBS when they could have received higher compensation elsewhere. They embraced their roles in the spirit of service to others and their commitment is what shines through on a daily basis. Their *seva* (service) was recognized by Sant Ji when he visited the school and ashram for the last time in 1996. Speaking to the school community (along with a couple of thousand guests) under a circus tent on the playing field, he concluded, *"I appreciate the teachers who are teaching here. There are many who have been teaching here for a very long time, even though I know that here they are not paid very much salary… I have much appreciation and respect for their seva which they are doing here for the children."*[126]

In the fall of 2013 the board of trustees recognized a particular group of faculty members for their long-time dedication to the

---

[125] Original trustees were Ursula Allen (parent), Richard Cardozo (friend and subsequent faculty), Anne Chase (parent), Jon Engle (faculty), Shepard Erhart (friend and subsequent parent), Tracy Leddy (friend), Mildred Meeh (faculty), Russell Perkins (faculty and former parent), Robert Schongalla (faculty and parent), Whit Smith (friend), Robert Upton (friend and parent) and Anne Wiggins (friend). Charlie and Sally Boynton (friends) attended as guests from the beginning, and Susan Dyment (faculty and parent) served as secretary for over thirty years.

[126] Talk given July 24, 1996 at Sant Bani School. See the Appendix for the full talk.

school. The seven teachers were designated as constituting "The Founders Group," defined as follows:

> **The Founders Group:** This group is made up of the seven Satsangis who devoted their entire professional lives to the building of an educational institution with a bright future: Susan Dyment, Robert Schongalla, Jonathan Powell, Debbie Asbeck, Jon Engle, and Kent and Karen Bicknell. For many years this group had no health care and worked for less than minimum wage, without the benefit of retirement assistance during the most important years of their careers. They poured their enthusiasm and love into the Masters' School and asked for little in return. Hundreds of children and their families benefitted from an education they could not have afforded without the financial sacrifice of these founding teachers. We must honor their loyalty while also preparing for the future with new teachers and leaders who will carry on the great work of the School.[127]

While the Founders Group may be unique, there are dozens of teachers and staff members who worked at SBS twenty, or even thirty, years and more. These dedicated professionals helped shape many facets of the school and deserve everyone's gratitude for all that they gave and, in some cases, continue to contribute.

Changing Demographics, Changing Times

Shortly after the turn of the millennium independent day schools were advised to pay careful attention to the shifting demographics of the areas they served. The economic downturn of 2008 accentuated this issue as in central New Hampshire both the number of school-age children and the ability of families to afford tuition began to drop. These forces impacted SBS, especially the high school division. At the same time, choices for local adolescents increased as public schools improved and independent schools offered more financial aid to attract day students. These factors combined with a shift in what many families were looking for at the secondary level. Prospective students wanted the choice of a broad array of academics (such as Mandarin and/or Russian along with French and Spanish) and elite sports programs.

---

[127] Meeting of the Board of Trustees on Oct 19, 2013.

As the high school population began to dwindle the school accepted how critical it was to re-evaluate its priorities. To better understand current and future trends in the school's locale and to guide it through a strategic planning process, the board of trustees hired an outside firm with much expertise in this area.[128] After several months of gathering data and analysis it became clear that Sant Bani School should focus all of its resources on becoming a "best-in-class" elementary school. To move forward as a K-8 program only was a challenging and emotional step on many levels, and the decision to do so included excitement about the future coupled with sadness for what was lost. While the school was returning to its roots, it was also closing a part of the school that had been so important to so many for almost forty years.

The executive director of the Commission on Independent Schools,[129] Jay Stroud, followed with much interest the school's strategic process at this juncture. His reflection, after spending a day on campus in May of 2016, captures well what the school went through.

> From the 'professional' perspective, it is clear that Sant Bani has made an exceptionally well-thought-out and carefully executed 're-focusing' of the program. You have decided the programs you can sustain and those you cannot and have taken some necessary—and I am sure sometimes exceptionally difficult— steps to achieve them. If my goal for the day was simply being assured that the future of the School, as far as can be determined, was bright and optimistic, that was achieved without question. I understand there are a host of challenges ahead, but by focusing on a new financial model, eliminating the upper school, paring the staff, making major renovations to key facilities and looking to the future of leadership within the School, you are preparing deliberately and intelligently for the future.[130]

---

[128] Ian Symonds and Associates (http://iansymmonds.org/)
[129] The Commission on Independent Schools (CIS) is one of four divisions of the New England Association of Schools and Colleges (NEASC), the accrediting organization for SBS.
[130] Jay Stroud, email to author, May 15, 2016.

Our hope was to continue to live up to the challenge Sant Ji put before a group of SBS faculty in India in March of 1983. While walking through the fields of Rajasthan, he paused and said, *"Ever since I have been to your school it has been my hearty desire – and still it is there – that the day should come when your school should become #1 in your area. And people from far and near should always have this desire: to send their children in your school. And even children studying in the other schools should have the desire of coming and studying in your school. That can only happen if all of you will work hard."*

It is interesting that Sant Ji outlined some criteria for measuring success: that families "from far and near" would want their children at SBS and that students in other schools would wish to transfer. These markers continue to be met as more and more families discover the school and students who visit frequently wish they could transfer at once. It is a moving experience to see Sant Ji's hopes for SBS be realized year after year.

****

Conclusion: *Be Good. Do Good. Be One.*

Throughout his life Master Kirpal stressed how important it was for people everywhere to understand that all life is connected. This essential unity was a core message in his teachings. As he wrote in 1959, *"My goal is that of oneness. I spread the message of oneness in life and living. This is the way to peace on earth. This is the mission of my life, and I pray that it may be fulfilled."*[131] The mission of Sant Bani School, refined over the years through living out the educational principles laid down by Master Kirpal Singh and Sant Ajaib Singh, has always reflected this goal of oneness. This is perhaps captured best in the school's vision statement, which comes directly from Master Kirpal: *Be Good. Do Good. Be One.*[132]

The spiritual teachers who founded SBS did not "invent" the idea that all life is interconnected. This is a universal truth that often manifests when diverse people listen to and learn from each other. The worth of each individual is recognized, nourished and honored

---

[131] Master Kirpal Singh, "Birthday Message," 1959.
[132] This was a phrase Master Kirpal used often, including as noted in Chapter I when he wrote it on the card for students and staff at *Manav Vidya Mandir.*

at the same time that everyone is expected to contribute to the good of the community. SBS was, of course, not the first school to educate children in this sympathetic manner, as the approach has manifested again and again through the ages. Examples may be seen in the two articles in the Appendix about the 19th century New England Transcendentalists, Henry David Thoreau, Ralph Waldo Emerson, Louisa and Bronson Alcott, Elizabeth Peabody and Margaret Fuller, as well as in 1973 in the woods of central New Hampshire. From the beginning, Sant Bani School was grounded in a perspective that recognized the unity of life, and in its first few years developed a pedagogy in harmony with that worldview.[133]

While this final chapter on the foundational years of Sant Bani School is coming to a close, certainly many new and exciting chapters lie ahead. Establishing and supporting the school was important to the two spiritual teachers involved with it. On several occasions, Master Kirpal observed that the world needed a new type of school; that it needed the fruits of a "New Education." For over twenty years, Sant Ji endorsed and guided SBS while expressing the desire that it have a strong future. Speaking to the school community in 1990, he began by stating:

> As all of you know, this school started as a very small thing founded by my great Satguru, my great Master Kirpal Singh Ji. He had this wish that all the children who would come to this school, would get the correct and right education and that they would grow up as good citizens and help the community and the nation.
>
> You know that if any work has been started by a father — after he leaves, the wise children carry on the work of their father because it becomes their responsibility. Only they can be called as the wise children who continue working according to what their father taught them.

---

[133] See, for example, the note in my 1975 SBS journal cited in Chapter II: "*If we have got anything to say, let's put it right out front. Unity, unity, unity; love of All in all — how can we get it in school? How, so it carries over? 'Sant Bani School is dedicated to the CONCRETE REALIZATION of HUMAN UNITY.' How to achieve? How to come at it more from that point of view — in all areas — math, natural sciences, history, literature — unity in different modes?*"

Now the school has progressed very much and I am very grateful to all the dear ones who have donated and those who have worked very hard in making the school a success.[134]

As we strive to be good... to do good... and to be one, may we all pitch in to make the future of Sant Bani School even brighter than its past.

****

One More Outside Perspective

Sant Bani Ashram Links East and West
by Robert Kinerk and Dick Shetler
Lakes Region Trader, February 28, 1979

SANBORNTON – Nine-year-old Chris Bicknell grabbed his hockey stick Tuesday to join classmates behind the school for a fast, informal, hard-fought game. Norwegian sweater. Two-toned toque. A goalie with a baseball glove. The shrill calls of teammates and the crack of stick hitting stick. All the elements of a Yankee boy's winter afternoon are there.

Thursday, Chris and his family will board a Lufthansa airliner. First stop will be Frankfurt. From there the plane will carry them to India. In Delhi, friends have arranged for a bus. The bus will take Chris and his family to the northwestern state of Rajasthan.

Dust. Jungle. Camels. Wild dogs. Burlap bag carpets and on a wicker chair trimmed with bicycle tires, Sant Ajaib Singh Ji. All the elements of the East. All the elements of a spirit disdainful of material things. All the elements of a belief that the seeker of truth can conquer anger, aggression, disappointment and the many other perils man is heir to.

A serene establishment in Sanbornton, Sant Bani Ashram,

---

[134] Sant Ajaib Singh to the Sant Bani School Community, July 22, 1990. The full talk is in the Appendix.

links the two worlds.

"If you are looking for an overall explanation of ashram I would say it is a place of spiritual retreat," Kent Bicknell, Chris's father, says. Bicknell is principal at the ashram school. Nine full-time teachers instruct 55 students there in all the traditional subjects—English, history, science, algebra, Spanish, and French—and guide them toward simplicity, cooperation, reverence for life and dedication to the ideal of service to others.

The ashram exists as a place for meditation. It has attracted to Sanbornton, Franklin, Tilton, Meredith and other central New Hampshire towns a host of followers of Kirpal Singh and his successor Ajaib Singh Ji. The school on the ashram grounds serves the children of these followers. It also welcomes children whose parents have no commitment to the teachings of the Indian Masters.

"We started with six children in my house," Bicknell explains. "I was the only teacher." He has a BA from Yale, a Masters from Goddard and work in progress on a doctorate at Boston University to back up his teaching credentials. "At that time we were building this particular Stone Building." His office is a cubbyhole in a handsome building of natural fieldstone set gently into the slope of the field behind the old Perkins farm. "I thought at that time the Stone Building would last for 25 years, but by the third year we had to build this other part." In the newer addition, kindergartners on the carpet learning right-hand, left hand skills. Upstairs, high school students are putting the finishing touches on a cooperatively written musical play.

Bicknell is at work with Don Booth of Community Builders in Canterbury now designing a 20,000-sq. ft. addition to the school. The addition will be solar heated in a unique, original way. It will rise inside an envelope of glass and wood, as if it were in a box. The thermal envelope around the building will trap the strength of the sun. It will channel it down to a storehouse of stones. It will help tap the constant warmth of the earth.

To help finance the addition, the school, which has survived six years on tuition payments and donations, will begin a more active fund raising program. "Every week we sort of pray and open the mail," Bicknell says of the school's finances. Tuition charges, on paper are $1,200 a year, but scholarships and other financial aid reduce that for almost everyone at the school. "Now we are going to be a little more organized with our capital expansion drive." [135]

A new bus to cut down on traffic to and from the school also looms large in Bicknell's growth plans. Concern for the feelings of his neighbors on Osgood Road lies behind that purchase. Osgood Road cut through hundreds of calm country acres. A bit of that acreage is visible from the slope where Bicknell stands talking to visitors. He has tossed on the tattered maroon jacket with "New Hampton" spelled out on its back. His ties go back to New Hampton, the town and the school. The town and the school and the hockey team.

Out of sight up the slope, nine-year-old Chris lines up a shot on the goal. Crack! Tomorrow, India… the master… spiritual growth. How do you reconcile a commitment to humility, simplicity, and constant sounding of the inner life with hat tricks, slap shots, and the competitive pressure of hockey, Bicknell is asked.

He digests the question and considers the answer before making his reply. "We asked the master that. I had no trouble with it, but others wanted to know. He replied — and this has always been my belief — that athletics are valuable. It would seem to me sheltering if we avoided the situations hockey can give rise to. Any sort of lifetime path takes strength and courage, and experiences gained on the playing field can help teach us that."

Life is an unending process of learning.
Sant Ajaib Singh

---

[135] This construction also did not happen as the school acquired two neighboring properties and converted the residences to much-needed classroom space.

Appendix

Messages from Master Kirpal Singh

"Toward the New Education"[136]

Man has been regarded as the crown and glory of this creation. "Not only is man at the origin of development, not only is he its instrument and beneficiary, but above all he must be regarded as its justification and end." Man, as Lord Jesus told us, whom God made in His own image, should prove a worthy recipient of His blessings. But alas! the man of today has belied most of our expectations. Increasingly, his vanity has led him to regard himself as the center of the world, and made him oblivious of his shortcomings. The education system which could have remedied all ailments and promoted his all-round development has proved woefully inadequate. Somehow a student of today is unable to get true knowledge which could have helped him to acquire the right understanding of life resulting in right thoughts, right speech and right action. In fact, the real aim of education is to develop the character and individuality of a pupil, his mind, will and soul power. The best education is that which teaches us that the end of knowledge is service.

This service is another name for love and fellowship, which constitute the very essence of personal and social life. Love and fellowship bring with them peace, gentleness and humility, basic values of life whose significance has been repeatedly stressed by the sages and prophets of India and the world. To nurture these values, to practice them, and to adopt them wholeheartedly in life, is what is known as Spirituality. "Spirituality" is not a name of a few religious dogmas. In fact, there is no room for dogmatic assertion in

---

[136] As noted at the start of Chapter I, this talk was given by Master Kirpal Singh Ji at the official inauguration of the *Manav Kendra* Education Scheme, June 21, 1972, and was published in *Sat Sandesh* in September 1972. *Manav Kendra* was the potentially self-sufficient ideal community, dedicated to man-making, man service and land service, that Kirpal Singh established near Dehra Dun in the foothills of the Himalayas, and the school there (*Manav Vidya Mandir* or "Temple of Human Knowledge") was one of its most important parts.

spiritual life. Once Huen Tsang put a question to Shil Bhadra, the head of the Nalanda University: "What is Knowledge?" He replied, "My child, Knowledge is perception of the principles of laws of life. And the best principle of life is fellow-feeling — sharing with others what you have." He says that those who cook food for themselves alone are thieves. Jesus once asked his disciples, "What does it profit a man if he gains the whole world and loses his own soul?" The voice in them which brought forth the answer, "None, Jesus, none," was the voice of Spirituality. The tenth Guru says, "Those who put food in the mouths of the poor and the needy, they put it in my mouth."

This capacity to share is known as Spirituality, without which all education is a sheer exercise in futility. As Gentile, a great thinker, says, "A school without a spiritual content is an absurdity." Modern education is largely egocentric and makes men spiritually and socially incompetent; and they enter life with a view to gaining money on earth and applause for their own personal enjoyment, forgetting that true happiness begins only when one goes out of one's little self — the ego — and seeks the larger Self.

The most important thing about education is its relation to life. "Knowledge without action is empty as a shadow." "Education is not a withered parchment but the Living Water of the Spirit." The school should be a home of teachers and students who reflect in their studies, and on the playground and in their daily lives, the cherished virtue of humility. Till our knowledge enables us to imbibe the noblest things of life, it has not served its purpose. Al-Ghazali, a man of scholarship and meditation, says in his book *Child*, "Know, my child, that knowledge without action is insanity, and the noblest action is service."

The chief malady of current education is that it results in the disassociation of heart and head. It lays emphasis on the development of head, and does sharpen the intellect to some extent. But more essential is the liberation of the heart. That will be done when the reason is awakened in sympathy for the poor, the weak and the needy. Sacrifice grows out of the heart, so the heart is required to be unfolded.

The young should: (1) strive after the ideal of sacrifice and not emotions; (2) be simple, for simplicity is strength; (3) learn to cooperate with all, and not let differences in creed or political opinions stand in the way of solidarity; (4) accept the creative ideal, which regards humanity as one and service as the end of all knowledge. Teachers should train students in the spirit of sympathy and love, blending information with inspiration and knowledge with love. A man may pass university examinations and yet remain ignorant of the realities of life. He may have read a thousand books, yet be no better than a boor. But true education will make him truly cultured; and the soul of culture is courtesy. Scholarship may be proud; culture is humble.

Paradoxically enough, culture and agriculture are similar in many ways. The soul's *Kshetra* [field] must be cultivated by disciplining desires and emotions. Who could have put it better than Buddha who, while dilating on the analogy, observed, "I plow and sow and grow, and from my plowing and sowing I reap immortal fruit. My field is religion; the weeds I pick up are passions; my plow is wisdom; my seed is purity"? Our Rishis have prayed, *Tamso ma Jyotirgamaya* ("Lead me from darkness to light").

But this darkness cannot be illumined in just a day. Bricks, mortar, comforts and luxuries cannot give any such training. It is the proper atmosphere which can deliver the goods; that is why emphasis in the school should be on atmosphere more than on rules, textbooks and buildings.

The tender heart of a child calls for very delicate handling. In fact, education begins even before birth and therefore better care must be bestowed upon every pregnant mother. It is a constant association with gentle forces which breeds virtuous persons. A child is the center of creative life. It needs to be opened as a flower is opened, gently, by sympathy, not by force. Do not let the child be imprisoned in the examination machine; never let him be snubbed and scolded.

The fruits of fellowship are four-fold. The first fruit is *Artha*, which indicates the economic aspect of education. The second is *Dharma*, which preaches reverence for law. *Kama* provides for the freer and fuller growth of human beings. The most important is, of course, *Moksha*, the complete liberation. This is liberation from our petty selves, which impels us to shed all our bigotry, narrow-mindedness, and chauvinism. If education does not enable us to raise ourselves from the levels of our ordinary selves, our average minds

126

to heights above our normal vision, it does not fulfill its very purpose. It is a lamentable fact that present education, which should insure an integrated growth of human personality, provides a very incomplete and insufficient preparation for life.

In this process, the situation of the school also plays a major role. The German word *kindergarten* is quite suggestive in this context. *Kinder* means child, and *garten* garden, indicating that every school should be situated in a lovely spot of nature. In ancient India, every Ashram was a garden of nature. The *Manav Kendra* is situated at a healthy and picturesque spot in the Doon Valley, presenting a glorious and tempting view of the snow-clad peaks of the Himalayas. In the true tradition of *Manav Kendra* — the Man Center — it belongs to all mankind for creation of understanding, peace and progress. The institution is dedicated to the concrete realization of human unity and is projected as an entirely new concept of integral education and moral living according to the ethics of spirituality. Human body is the true Temple of God. God resides in the temple of the body made by Him in the womb of the mother, and not in the temples made by the hands of man. Without an inner change, man can no longer cope with the all-round development of his life. To accomplish this vital and indispensable task, the very nature of education has to be transformed so that it can give society young men and women who are not only intellectually but emotionally trained for vigorous, realistic and constructive leadership. We envisage such an atmosphere where persons will be able to grow and develop integrally without losing contact with their souls.

The aim is to make it a place where the needs of the spirit and concern for human progress will take precedence over material satisfactions, pleasures and enjoyment. Certainly the education will have to be spiritually oriented and given, not with a view to passing examinations, getting certificates and diplomas, and seeking employment, but for enriching the existing moral, ethical and other faculties and opening up new vistas and horizons to fulfill the dream of Reality.

"On the Unity of Man"[137]

MAN, the highest rung of all creation, is basically the same everywhere. All men are born the same way, receive all the bounties of nature in a similar manner, have the same inner and outer construction, and are controlled in the physical body by the same Power, called differently as "God," "Word," *Naam*, etc. All men are the same as souls, worship the same God, and are conscious entities; being of the same essence as God, they are members of His family, and thus related to each other as brothers and sisters in Him.

All awakened and enlightened Gurus and spiritual teachers who came to this world at various points of time and in various parts, have invariably emphasized this Truth in their own language and manner. According to them all men, despite their distinctive social orders and denominational religions, form but one class.

Guru Nanak, the great teacher and Messiah of peace, said:

The highest order is to rise into Universal brotherhood;
Aye, to consider all creation your equal.

India's ancient mantra, *Vasudeva kutumb bukam*, also lays down the same principle that the whole world is one family. However, it is common knowledge that despite long and loud preaching by various religious and social leaders professing the Unity of Man, the world today is torn by strains and tensions of every kind, and presents a sorrowful spectacle indeed. More often than not we see individuals at war with one another and brothers at drawn daggers with their own kith and kin. Similarly, nations are constantly involved in conflicts and clashes with each other, thus spoiling the peace and tranquility. It seems that the root cause of this present-day situation is, that the Gospel of Unity of Man, however well accepted in theory, has not struck home to humanity at large and is not put into practice. It is only a form of slogan-mongering done

---

[137] Issued on May 15, 1974, "On the Unity of Man" is the last of Master Kirpal Singh's "circular letters" to his initiates. As throughout his works, "man" is translated from the original Hindi/Urdu word, *insan*, which means "human being." Hindi and Urdu use different scripts but share many, many words. The Hindi word is इन्सान.

with calculated motives.

It is universally accepted that the highest purpose of this human body is to achieve union of the soul with the Oversoul or God. It is on this account that the physical body is said to be the True Temple of God wherein He Himself resides. All religions spell out the ways and means of meeting the Oversoul or God; and all the ways and means so suggested, however different looking, lead to the same destination, so that one need not change from one religion to another for this purpose. One has only to steadfastly and genuinely tread upon the lines drawn by the torchbearers for achieving the goal.

It is necessary, however, that greater effort should be made toward the realization of Unity of Man. We have to realize that every human being is as much a member of the brotherhood as we are, and is obviously entitled to the same rights and privileges as are available to us. We must therefore make sure that while our own children make merry, our neighbor's son does not go without food; and if we really practice this, much present-day conflict will be eliminated. Each of us will develop mutual recognition, respect and understanding for the other, thus wiping out the gross inequities of life. In this process, as the mutual recognition and understanding develops, it becomes a vital force generating a reservoir of fellow feeling which in turn will bring culture and ultimately humility — the basic need of the hour.

The holding of the World Conference on Unity of Man in February 1974 in New Delhi was a clarion call to the world. This conference was perhaps the first of its kind since the time of Ashoka the Great, held at the level of Man with the noble purpose of fostering universal brotherhood leading to universal harmony. This message of the Unity of Man must reach every human heart irrespective of religious and social labels so that it comes home to every individual, enabling him to actually put it in practice in life and pass it on to others; in this way, the entire human society could be reformed. Truly speaking, Unity already exists: as man — born in the same way, with the same privileges from God; and as soul — a drop of the Ocean of All Consciousness called God, Whom we worship by various names; but we have forgotten this Unity. The lesson has only to be revived.

129

The so-called worldwide campaign for Unity of Man is not intended to affect the existing social and religious orders in any manner. In fact, each one has to continue to work for the upliftment of man in its own way as before. Additionally, however, this campaign has to carry the clarion call of Unity of Man to as large a mass of humanity through its own vehicle as it can, so that the message cuts across the barriers of misunderstanding and mutual distrust and strikes home to every human heart. Further, the said campaign has to be carried out not by intellectual wrestling, but with optimum desire and anxiety to put the Unity of Man into practice so that it becomes a real living force. The method of propagation has to be by self-discipline and self-example rather than by declaration and proclamations.

It would be prudent to clarify that the campaign of Unity of Man has to be carried out above the level of religions without in any way affecting any religious or social orders. It has to obtain in practice the blessings and support of all those who believe in the Gospel of Unity of Man, and could give it strength by taking this Gospel to every human heart around them and convincing them of the need of its acceptance in daily life. It will neither be tagged with Ruhani Satsang nor with any other similar organization. The enthusiasm of its admirers will be the real force working behind the campaign.

It is therefore earnestly requested that all those who believe in the Unity of Man and wish to carry its message must work ceaselessly so that it may reach the lonest corner of the world.

A World Conference on Unity of Man may be arranged in the West as was done at Delhi in the East — both ultimately work as one whole.

Sant Ajaib Singh's Addresses
to the Sant Bani School Community

"Address to the SBS Community" May 1977[138]

"Education and Discipline" July 1980[139]

I am very glad to see all of you. Most of the dear ones I know personally, because they have come around the ashram and are initiates and I have seen them many times, and I have met their children also. But some of the dear ones whom I have never met before, I've got this opportunity to see them. So I'm very grateful and I'm very pleased to see all the dear ones. I welcome all of you, and I appreciate that all of you have come here to listen to me.

All those who are learned, they already know how important it is to study to get an education, and what the benefits of education are. And you know what we have to sacrifice and what we have to do in order to get a better education.

We know that the most important thing for every child in the building of his educated life is school. It is the stepping-stone of the life of the children, so if the school is good and if the teachers are good, only then can the children get good education from the very beginning. When they grow older and go to college they will be able to understand things much better.

Saints are also like teachers. As the teachers teach the children in the school what is good and what is bad, in the same way, when the Master Saints come in this world they also start their school, which we ordinarily call "Satsang." You can call it "Satsang" or "school," and in that satsang or school Masters lovingly tell us what is good for us and what is bad for us. They tell us what things we should do to improve our life and what things we should not do, so that we may make our life much better... Even though some people come to the Masters when they are fifty years old, some when they are forty years old, when they first come they are all like children. They don't know anything.

---

[138] This talk was printed in its entirety in Chapter IV.
[139] Sant Ji gave this talk to the students, parents and faculty of Sant Bani School on Sunday, July 13, 1980.

In the same way, the children who have joined the school don't know anything. They don't even know how to sit, how to stand, how to talk. They don't even know how much respect and appreciation they should have for the teacher. Whereas those who come to the Path don't know anything about the glory of the Master, but at least they know how to deal with people. But children don't even know that. Children don't even know that the education which they are getting will be helpful for them in the future and that because of a good education they will make a good life. Children are innocent and they don't know that this thing is good for them.

In such a situation the parents are the first teachers of the children. So if the parents tell the children, "Dear children, it is good for you to go to school, and after going to school it is good for you to study wholeheartedly, and respect the teachers and remain in the discipline," only then can the children have a better understanding about the importance of going to school. Because school is a totally new thing for them, they don't know how to utilize their time in the best way. So that is why it becomes so very important for the parents to teach the children about the importance of the school and how to behave there. If they tell all these things to the children it will be helpful for them.

Children are the wealth of nations. The leaders, emperors, kings and great people of the future will come up from these children only, so it is very important for us to give them a good education. If they do not study in a correct way, then how can they progress in life? More than that — how can they help in the progress of the country? If we will teach the children to be in discipline, we will help the teachers of the school. If the children will remain in discipline, the teachers will be able to put all their attention on the children and love them. And when the children remain in discipline and receive so much love and respect from the teachers, they will appreciate that, and they will be able to learn more.

So that is why it is very important for us to remember these things: first of all, we should have respect for the school to which our children are going, and the children also should have respect for their school. After that comes respect and appreciation for the teachers. If the children respect and appreciate the teachers, they will gain a lot. And if the parents teach the children about discipline and teach discipline to them, it will be helpful in their studies also.

In Rajasthan there was one Swami Keshvanand, and he established one school. He encouraged people to give donations, he raised a lot of funds, and he worked very hard to establish that school. And when it was established many children got educated, and it was very well respected in the area. That school produced many good leaders, and many became well known, because they had been given a very good education. Many even became Members of Parliament, which is not a small thing in India. But later on those who had gotten an education there didn't remember the school, nor have any respect for it. That affected the new generation, who also started not respecting the school, and in that way the name of the school went down and down.

So once Swami Keshvanand invited all the old students. Among those who came were many Members of Parliament, ministers, etc. The Swami told them "Don't you remember the education you got from this school? You have become Members of Parliament only because of that education. Should you not take care of the school?" Education is the first thing which makes our life. If we are illiterate we cannot deal with people, we cannot earn anything; we cannot do anything if we don't have a good education. He meant to say that, to whichever school our children are going, we should have respect for that school, and we should always help it in whatever way we can.

Master Sawan Singh never forgot His teacher, even though Master Sawan Singh became a Param Sant. Still He always remembered His teacher and whenever He met him He gave him much respect.

Swami Keshvanand had been a Member of Parliament when India became independent. At that time most of the Members of Parliament and leaders were illiterate. He felt very bad about that and that's why he was inspired to start such a school. He went from one village to another, from door to door, collecting money for the school, and he worked hard for many years; eventually he was successful. Swami Keshvanand used to say that those who don't help the schools, but who always criticize the schools where their children are going, are doing no good for their children... He used to say that such people are the enemies of society, because they don't appreciate the place from where the leaders of the future are going to come.

Swami Keshvanand was a very simple man who ate simple food. But he used to work very hard for the benefit of other people. And you know that when someone is working selflessly for other people, the worldly people think that he is not in his senses, that he is a madman. So people used to taunt him, saying, "We will see if this hard work that you are doing will bear any fruit." Swami Keshvanand said, "Don't worry about me. Whatever work I am doing, definitely will prove worthwhile. It will benefit the people. I don't want to die while lying on my bed—I want to die while I am still active." It so happened that when he left his body, he was still very much in action, even though he was very old. He left the body in Delhi while he was walking.

If somebody donates money to a school, and if the children study wholeheartedly, and become worthwhile people, then you can see whose donation has made that possible.

In India there are six deeds which are considered most holy. One is to give donations in the name of God; another is to receive donations in the name of God for God's work; the third is to give education; the fourth is to receive the education of God; the fifth is to perform the devotion of the Lord, and the sixth is to make other people do the devotion of God.

In India in the old days people used to teach children with the understanding that they were giving the donation of knowledge to the children, and the children used to have so much respect and appreciation for their teachers that they used to call them "gurus," or "masters." Those who studied in those early schools, even if they went up to the fourth grade only, still had much more discipline and knowledge than the masters and graduates of this time, because nowadays, if the teachers are strict—and sometimes they have to be strict—the children rebel and don't like it. And when the teachers are not appreciated and respected by the children, they also think, "Why should we bother so much for the children? We will get paid anyway!" But this is not good for the children or for the teachers.

It is the duty of the parents to teach discipline to the children. If we teach them discipline, it will be good and helpful for the teachers in the schools. Moreover, by doing that we are having mercy on our children. If we teach them discipline, and how to remain in discipline, it will help them here in this school and when they go to other schools, and when they do their work when they go into the world. Everywhere they will find it very helpful.

In childhood everybody's mind is very swift—like a monkey. Little children always have very fast thoughts, and they love to think about how to fool the teacher and play mischief. You know that children love to get many days off from school so they can play and do whatever they want. Once it so happened that there were some children who wanted to have a day off to play, so all of them decided to play a trick on the teacher. When the teacher came into the classroom one boy got up and said, "Sir, why do you look so sad and weak today?" But the teacher said, "No, I don't have any problem, I am okay. You go and sit down." But another child got up and said, "No, sir, you should believe us—your face is very pale. Something is wrong with you. Are you sick?" He answered, "No, no, no, no. I'm all right, you go and sit down. Let us start the work." But the other one got up and said, "No, sir. You should rest today. You definitely need to rest, because if you don't rest you will get sicker." And in that way, since all the children told him, he was convinced somehow that he was sick and that he should go and rest.

But he was also very smart. So he said, "Okay. You all come with me to my home, and I will lie down in bed, and you come with me and read there. If you want me to rest, I will rest." So he took them home and, because he was convinced that he was sick, he started arguing with his wife. He said to her, "You are supposed to take good care of my health. You didn't tell me that I was weak and pale; the children told me. You are not giving me good food and care!" She said, "No, you are all right. You are normal." But he said, "No, you are lying."

Anyway, he lay down on the bed and he had all the children sitting near him. Now the children thought, "We played this trick because we wanted a day off, but the teacher is very smart. He told us to come here and still we don't have the day off." So they thought of playing one more trick. They said to each other, "Let us read very loudly, and when we read aloud then maybe he will get a headache and tell us to go." So they started reading loudly. After some time the teacher got upset and he said, "Don't make me have a headache. You go. Today is a day off."

So children are very much like this. They always want many days off because they like to play. But if we tell them how important it is for them to go to school regularly, attend their classes, and study wholeheartedly — if we teach them discipline — that will be helpful for them.

"Children are the Wealth of the Nation" July 1990[140]

I am very pleased to be able to come here and to be among all of you. In my past tours, I have seen many of the families who are here; and now I am happy to see the new families joining the group.

As all of you know, this school started as a very small thing and it was founded by my great Satguru, my great Master Kirpal Singh Ji. He founded this school for the benefit of the children and for the benefit of the community over here. He had this wish that all the children who would come to this school, would get the correct and right education and that they would grow up as good citizens and help the community and the nation.

You know that if any work has been started by a father — after he leaves, the wise children carry on the work of their father because it becomes their responsibility. Only they can be called as the wise children who continue working according to what their father taught them.

Satguru Master Kirpal Singh Ji used to say that it is not the Masters Themselves Who make Themselves famous, it is Their disciples Who make Them famous. Because if the disciples will live and follow the teachings of the Masters, if they will make their own character good and if they will present a good example to other people in the world, then they will be glorifying the name of their Master.

Even on a worldly level the same thing applies. If your children are good and they have done good things in the world, they will be glorifying the name of their parents.

Now the school here has progressed very much and I am very grateful to all the dear ones who have donated and those who have worked very hard in making the school a success. Kent Bicknell has

---

[140] This talk was given to students, teachers, parents and alumni of Sant Bani School, on Sunday, July 22, 1990.

always been talking to me about the progress of the school whenever he comes to Rajasthan, where I live; he always talked about things at the school and I am grateful to all the dear ones who have helped him to make the school a success.

No wealth of this world — nothing of this world goes with us. When we leave this body, when we leave this world, not even the body in which we are sitting now and we claim to be our very own, goes with us. We have to leave everything here. But all the good deeds we have done — and if we have helped other people to achieve something good — only those things remain in this world and those things always shine and our name is also shining and we are always glorified in this world if we have done good things like that. Master Sawan Singh Ji used to say, "When people leave this world, they leave behind their name. If they have done good things — whatever they have done for the other people, since many people get benefit from the deeds of those people — they are always remembered. And those people who have donated for the good cause, or those who have worked for the good cause, they always continue getting the spiritual benefit."

Children are the wealth of the families. They are the wealth of the society and their local community and they are the wealth of the nation. When they grow up, from among them may come the ones who will be the best citizens of the country. And it is possible that some of them may rule over the country or take care of the affairs of the country. So if they have been brought up with the right education, if right from the beginning they have been given the right kind of education and if they grow up as very good citizens, then it will not only glorify the name of their families or community or society in which they have grown up, but it will also glorify the name of their country.

Saints always encourage us to glorify the name of our parents, to glorify the name of our families. They also inspire us to glorify the name of the society in which we are living and They always tell us to do things which will bring glory to the name of our country so that the people all over the world may know that such-and-such person is a citizen of that country.

We can do all these things only if our children will be given good education — only if they will be brought up in a good environment, only if they are taught the right discipline.

So once again I would like to extend my thanks and gratitude to all the dear ones, those who have contributed to making the school a success. In the future also it becomes the responsibility, especially of those dear ones whose children study in this school, to help the organizers, to help the people here and to contribute and work together with the dear ones here. Because you know that so far the school has grown so much—it has been very successful—and in the future also it is going to be more successful and many more children will come here and they will benefit from it. So it is the responsibility, especially of those parents whose kids come to this school, to help the people running the school by any way they can.

Kabir Sahib, a Saint, says, "If you get a lot of water in your boat, and in the same way, if you get a lot of money in your home, what is the wise thing to do? You should try to throw out that water with both hands. Otherwise you will get drowned." In the same way, if you have a lot of wealth, you should try to give it for the good cause.

Further He says, "You do not lose anything when you give for the good cause, just as the river does not go dry no matter how much water people take from it. If you don't believe me," He says, "You can try this for yourself."

Rajasthan, the place where I live, is much different now than what it used to be thirty-five years ago. The dear ones who have been to Rajasthan recently have seen how there are now good roads over there, there are trees everywhere and there is a lot of water there. But about thirty-five years ago, in Rajasthan there was not so much water, we did not have any good roads and there was no greenery at all.

There was a great Saint, a holy man in Rajasthan, who was elected as a member of the Parliament from Rajasthan. When he went around, touring the state of Rajasthan, he was surprised to see how many people in the state of Rajasthan were illiterate. He resigned from being a member of Parliament. He came down to Rajasthan and encouraging, inspiring people to give donations, He collected a lot of money and he founded a school. Later on He also opened an agricultural college. He used to say, "If God has given you a lot of wealth and you are not donating for the education of the illiterate, of the people, then it is better for you to wear a garland of stones and drown yourself in the water."

The schools and institutions which He founded became so popular and so good that many people took advantage of them and many of His students became members of Parliament or members of the local assembly; many of them became very good professionals and they are leading a very good life.

So, lovingly, all of you are requested that we should pay as much attention as possible towards the progress of this school, because it is our very own. It is like our own home, and we should always think about making it more successful, because we are the ones who are gaining from this school. We are the ones who are benefiting from the school, because it is our children who go to this school, and in the future also many more children will also come to this school.

When I came here on the first tour, at that time the school was very small and there were not so many big buildings of the school; but this time that I have come here, I am very happy to see the new school building, and to see all of you who have worked very hard and all those who have contributed in making that building. I was pleased to see that building and I am thankful to all those who have helped in making that building.

[Sant Ji asks Kent Bicknell, the principal, if he has anything he wishes to say. Kent thanks Sant Ji for coming here and visiting the school.]

I am also very thankful to all the dear ones, especially all the families who have come here, spending their precious time. I am very thankful to all of you who have come here.

"If We Take the Master Power With Us" July 1996[141]

Salutations unto the Feet of Supreme Fathers Lord Almighty Sawan and Kirpal, Who after coming to this earth have planted the plants of Their love. The plants of love which They planted now have grown up, and I'm very pleased to see those grown up plants. In 1977 when I came here for the first time the school didn't have

---

[141] Sant Ji gave this talk to an audience of 2000 gathered on the SBS Athletic Field on July 24, 1996. Students, parents and faculty were sitting at the front of the crowd.

many buildings and there were not so many teachers, and not so many students.

Kent Bicknell, the principal, has worked very hard. Without getting tired, he has taken along with him all the families which came along his way, all the students, all the teachers. He worked very hard. He kept me posted with every single thing which was happening at the school. And this is the reality, that if we take the Guru Power, the Master Power along with us, whatever work we do taking refuge at His Feet and taking the Master Power along with us, we definitely prosper and become successful in it. He has even kept me informed about the dear ones who have supported the school over the years—he has told me about them, and he has introduced me to them. And I have always appreciated them, and once again I would like to express my gratitude. I would like to thank them for all that they have done for the school.

Regarding the education, you know that those children who have passed this school and who have gone to the other schools for higher education, they have glorified the name of this school. And as you know, children are the wealth of the nation. They are the ones who are going to take care of the nation, the ones who are going to lead this nation and this society. So unless the children have a good education, unless their foundation is strong, they cannot be the leaders of society, they cannot run the nation. So in this school you know that a lot of emphasis is put upon building up the character and a good foundation is made for the children. In this school a lot has been taught about character and a good education is given so that when they go out to the other schools they glorify the name of this school. They can glorify the name of this school only if they have gotten a good education. So I am very pleased that the children who have gone to higher schools after finishing their schooling here have glorified the name of this school.

I hope that the families who have been helping will continue supporting the school and Kent Bicknell. I also hope that the children who are here for the education will get a good education and that when they go on to the other schools they will glorify the name of the school and they will also make their lives and glorify themselves.

Dear ones, you know that the Saints have all the qualities and They also have the quality of service to Their nation in abundance within Them. Wherever They are born They always do those things which glorify the name of Their nation. They always serve Their nation. You know that Master Sawan Singh and Master Kirpal Singh were born in India; They spread the seeds of *Naam* everywhere in the world. They did the meditation of *Naam* and They spread *Naam* everywhere whether it was the forest or the ocean or on the mountains. They took the message of *Naam* everywhere and only because of that now we are inclined towards India and we say that They have come from India. So the Saints have this quality of serving the nation and They teach that to all of us.

The other precious quality which the Masters have within them is service to the souls. They serve the souls, They do the meditation and They teach the souls what They have done Themselves by obeying the orders of Their Master. They do not let Their soul become dirty in the dirt of the worldly passions and pleasures and They do the devotion of God Almighty with Their soul and They teach us that and They make us do that. So They don't allow Themselves to be dirty in the dirt of this world. They always serve the souls. The qualities which the Masters have and what the Masters have taught us first, is that we should serve our nation, and then that we should serve the souls. We should always remember these qualities and we should try to be like Them.

The special message which I have for the students is that they should abstain from using drugs. You know that in the present time the use of drugs and intoxicants is spread everywhere, and it affects the body very badly. In the schools and colleges, students use drugs a lot, so that is why I would like to tell all the dear children that you should abstain from the drugs and the intoxicants because they have a very bad effect on your body, and that effect stays there for a long time in your life. It ruins your life. So that is why you should abstain from all kinds of drugs and intoxicants. I would also like to tell the dear teachers that they should explain to the students the bad effects of the drugs and intoxicants on their body. They should do this very lovingly...

Dear Children, this brief message which I have given to you, I have said that because I have much mercy for you. In my heart I have much sympathy and much love for you and that is why I have said this. I hope that you will appreciate this, that you will take advantage of this. I hope that you will abstain from the drugs and you will make your life pure and healthy.

In the end I would like to tell all the dear children who were in this school before and who have passed out of this school that they should maintain the discipline and maintain the teachings which they were taught over here. No matter where they are, no matter where they go, they should maintain the discipline, and they should always remember the teachings which they have received here. They should always remain connected with the Satsang so that they may glorify the name of this school. I would also like to tell Kent Bicknell that just as up until now he has taken along all the dear ones, all the families who have supported the school, in the same way, that he will continue doing this and that he will do all possible things to make this school successful.

I pray to Lord Almighty Kirpal that He may shower His grace upon all of you and that with His grace this school may progress by leaps and bounds and your soul may also come closer to God Almighty, that your soul may also progress.

I appreciate the teachers who are teaching here. There are many dear ones, many teachers who have been teaching here for a very long time, even though I know that here they are not paid very much salary, but they are doing this work as a *seva*, and I have much appreciation and respect for their *seva* which they are doing here for the children.

Sant Ajaib Singh's Graduation Messages: Excerpts

Class of 1983

You are entering into a new phase of your life. If you will remember the teachings of this school, I'm sure success will come to you in all things. I hope you will do such things in your life that not only your family but also your school may take pride in.

Class of 1984

I send all four of you heartiest congratulations and best wishes on this important day in your life. As you know, school is the stepping-stone which will help us throughout our lives. What you have learned up to now you should use for the benefit of others so as to be a credit to your family and your school. By helping others and making others happy, you yourself will become happy, as true happiness lies in the service of others. Whether you are going on to a college or university, or to some other work in the world, you should not forget your real purpose — to find the Supreme Lord within yourself. This is the highest service that you can do.

Class of 1987[142]

May Master's love and blessing be with you always. On this day I would like to congratulate all of you on the occasion of your graduating from Sant Bani School. I wish you all success in your lives.

As you know, now you have finished one phase of your life and are going to enter the second phase, which is more challenging and in which you will be exposed more to the world and its ways. Up until now you were in an environment filled with God's grace and Spirituality. Now you will go into a world of complete *Maya* (illusion) and distractions. So you will have to be more cautious. Since most of you are either Initiates or from Satsangi families I would like to advise you to always remember the teachings of the Path and to your best ability you should follow it. Sant Mat is a very practical Path. It is not a cult or any hypocrite religion. If you will

---

[142] The majority of students in this class began at Sant Bani in first grade and were from Satsangi families, as Sant Ji acknowledges in his message.

practice it in your daily lives you will receive much help in building your career.

Class of 1991

Dear children, you know that now when you will go to different colleges, you will have to meet many new people. The environment in which you will be living now will be much different from the environment of Sant Bani School. I hope that you will maintain your strength and the wisdom which you have received from attending this school, and meeting all the challenges in your life, that you will progress and prosper in your life.

Class of 1992

Hearty congratulations to each one of you! I join you and your family and the school in this celebration of coming closer to the perfection in your lives. This life is an unending process of learning. You are the very fortunate ones who get to learn the things of the world and also true lessons of spirituality at this school. I hope that you will not forget the education you have received here, and that it will always illuminate your path.

Throughout history the words of the Masters have proven to be timeless and true. Two thousand years ago, Jesus Christ taught, "Love, and all things shall be added unto you," and that Love is the light of this world. Similarly the ancient scriptures of India implore the Limitless God to lead us from darkness into light. "The highways and byways of this world are full of darkness; Lift up the torch of knowledge to light your way!" My best wishes and the blessings of the Master are always with you for your bright future.

Class of 1993

Dear children, the purpose of receiving the education is not just to become successful in the worldly fields such as trade, science, engineering, etc. It has a higher purpose and that is to get the right understanding. Masters say that the right understanding first lies in realizing God Almighty Who is the Maker of this universe and Who controls everything. So I hope that along with receiving the worldly education you will also make efforts to get the right understanding.

Class of 1994

Congratulations! I am very pleased that you have completed your studies at the Sant Bani School and are now ready to go on to college for higher studies. I wish you all the best with the hope that you may become successful in the world.

Dear children, I have only one piece of advice for you, and that is always maintain discipline and work hard. Never become lazy. Continue working hard until you reach your goal. You know that the power who misleads us is within us, and the power who encourages us to take the right path is also within us. So, develop the right understanding and do your best. The Almighty Lord and His Servants always teach us to be righteous. I hope that all of you will remember the good things you have learned at the Sant Bani School.

Class of 1995

Today you have finished the education program at the Sant Bani School and you should always remember the good teachings you have received here. It is important to use our knowledge and understanding for the benefit of others. We must recognize our own shortcomings and forgive others—in this way we will bring happiness not only to others but to our own selves also. And the Supreme Power within will also be pleased with us. Everyone appreciates the lovely fragrance coming from a flower.

Class of 1997

I wish that you will continue your studies in the best educational institutions and achieve success in your life. Remember that one can never learn enough—there is always something more to learn. So respect our teachers because they are the ones from whom you have to learn. Maintain a good character, and be receptive.

Writings on Thoreau, Emerson and the Alcotts

In a conversation with Sant Ji in March of 1994 I talked about the links between Sant Mat and the group of 19th-century New Englanders known as the Transcendentalists. I shared that Henry Thoreau, Ralph Waldo Emerson and Bronson Alcott, among others, were struck by the spiritual wisdom captured in ancient texts like *The Bhagavad Gita, The Upanishads* and the teachings of the Buddha. I said that, having come of age in the 1960s, it seemed like my generation had "invented" turning to India for inner guidance. The reality, however, was that we were following a well-worn trail blazed more than 125 years before by some of the greatest luminaries of American thought. I concluded by suggesting I write an article about this for *Sant Bani Magazine* as I thought Satsangis might find it inspiring.

The strength of Sant Ji's response surprised me. He said, "*It is very good that you are thinking of writing the article which you have mentioned. It will not only be a good thing for Satsangis to know, but also for the other non-Satsangis — those who are the present-day critics of the Path. For them also it will be a good thing to know. It is very good and I hope that it will help everyone.*"

Following this advice, I wrote (or co-wrote) two papers that touch directly on the many connections between the Transcendentalists and the Asian Wisdom Traditions as embodied in, for example, Buddhism and Hinduism: "Brooks and Ditches: A Transcendental Look at Education," and "The Asian Soul of Transcendentalism," both of which are below. Following their publication in widely-circulating magazines, I uploaded the articles to the web. They have now been viewed by readers in India, China, Russia, Vietnam, Turkey, Iran, Tunisia, Sri Lanka, Romania, Korea, Nepal, UAE, Austria, Netherlands, Singapore, Bangladesh, Israel, Kazakhstan, Poland, Mexico, Indonesia, France, Egypt, Italy, England, Denmark, Germany, Switzerland, Canada, Brazil, Australia, the Philippines and Colombia, as well as the United States.

"Brooks and Ditches:
A Transcendental Look at Education"[143]

Imagine the reaction if developers in your area took all of the natural streams and brooks, drained and dredged each one, and created ditches designed for a specific purpose that someone, somewhere, had decided would be for "the greater good." In a journal entry for October 1850, American philosopher, naturalist and mystic Henry David Thoreau recorded this thought about schooling in America: *What does education often do? It makes a straight-cut ditch of a free, meandering brook.* When I shared this nugget with organizational development expert Peter Senge, he wryly noted, "Well, that just about says it all, doesn't it?"

How did Thoreau safeguard the meandering spirits in his care? How were his friends and neighbors approaching education, particularly Bronson Alcott, Ralph Waldo Emerson, Elizabeth Peabody, and the members of Brook Farm, the 19th-century intentional community frequented by the Transcendentalists? Where did their ideas come from, and, more pertinently, do these century-and-a-half-old approaches have anything to offer schools today?

Education was of great interest to Emerson, Thoreau, Alcott, Peabody, and other Transcendentalists. They were energized by the classic dynamic of how to best integrate the individual and society, of how to create the ideal grounds for both to grow while simultaneously honoring both. Although there was much that the group did not agree on, at the heart of their approach lay two key principles: (1) a deep respect for one's self and the other; and (2) the adoption of core human values that led to efforts to build communities and/or shape society with those values as guideposts. To embrace these two required a perspective shift best achieved through stepping outside of one's ordinary "self." As Emerson noted late in his

---

[143] Published in the Fall 2008 issue of *Independent School Magazine*, Vol. 68, No. 1, National Association of Independent Schools (NAIS), Washington, D.C. pp. 82-88. Available on-line at https://www.nais.org/magazine/independent-school/fall-2008/brooks-and-ditches/

life, the entire era was a time when "the mind became aware of it-self."[144] From Emerson's perspective, this was a necessity for a young republic built on the premise that the people could govern themselves, for to govern oneself one first had to know one's self.

In 1834, Bronson Alcott opened an experimental school de-signed to help children know themselves. Alcott's Temple School was housed in the Masonic Temple on Tremont Street in downtown Boston. At the outset, the school was a radical departure from the typical New England educational experience. Like his fellow Tran-scendentalists, Alcott believed in the innate goodness of the child. He was fond of quoting Romantic poet William Wordsworth's con-viction that since we come into this world "trailing clouds of glory" it is only natural that "heaven lies about us in our infancy."[145] Al-cott's method of helping students recognize their own "goodness" relied on gentle guidance in aesthetically pleasant surroundings and a praxis built on conversations: questions and answers on a va-riety of topics (some of which later were viewed as too adult for mid-19th-century children). *Parley's Magazine*, a popular children's magazine of the day, offered young readers and their parents a snapshot of the Temple School with its carpeted floors, decorated walls, and comfortable chairs and sofas — a welcome contrast to the typically austere school of its day. "But what renders the school quite different," the magazine editor writes, "is that the pupils are taught to think and reason; and to talk about their thinking and feeling and reasoning. There are some little boys and girls there, scarcely six years old, who know how to think and reason about things as well as most men and women." Not surprisingly, the ed-itor also notes that most of the boys and girls "appear very happy."[146]

Not only were Alcott's students taught to "think and reason" but they were taught to *talk about* their own mental and emotional

---

144 Ralph Waldo Emerson in "Historic Notes of Life and Letters in New Eng-land," his hundredth lecture before the Concord Lyceum, in 1880. From *The Tran-scendentalists: the Classic Anthology*, Perry Miller, Editor (1950, renewed 1978, MJF Books, New York), p. 494.
145 William Wordsworth, "Ode: Intimations of Immortality from Recollections of Early Childhood" (1807).
146 An excerpt from "About Mr. Alcott's School," *Parley's Magazine*, November 1839 issue (Part XXVIII), pp. 131–132 (from the collection of the author).

processes. This is exactly the kind of self-reflective process that led Emerson to describe the era as one of self-awareness.

Caught up in the success of an educational environment that allowed children free rein to discuss a variety of topics, Alcott reasoned that the general public would embrace his approach. He asked his assistant (and classroom recorder) Elizabeth Peabody to prepare transcripts of the daily conversations for publication, but she warned against it, suggesting that Boston was not that enlightened yet. Alcott forged ahead. When the public opened Alcott's *Conversations on the Gospels* and discovered comments such as young Josiah Quincy's that children are born owing to people's "naughtiness put together to make a body for the child..." roars of outrage came from pulpit and press. Under societal pressure, parents removed their children, and when Alcott admitted a black child, most of those who had remained withdrew. Peabody was right. Boston, the Athens of America, was not ready to support a progressive educational venture, so Alcott closed the school. Thirty years later, after he had completed a successful stint as the superintendent of schools in Concord, Massachusetts, Alcott felt some vindication for his early vision when his star pupil from long ago, Josiah Quincy, remarked that the Temple School had been "the best thing attempted in modern times for a properly human culture."

Without the benefit of the Harvard education acquired by his friends Emerson and Thoreau, Bronson Alcott did much to create himself. After a brief stint in a clock factory and an aborted effort to gain entrance to Yale, he prepared for his career as an educator by taking to the road as a Yankee peddler, making several trips up and down the coast. As a northerner in the Deep South, Alcott was surprised when genteel homeowners opened their sitting rooms and libraries to him. He was an avid reader, hungry for knowledge. In his travels, he also connected with Quakers, whose simple message of inner light—every individual has a natural right to have a personal relationship with the Divine—resonated deeply.

It struck Alcott that children are born with that same inner light, not steeped in the "total depravity" preached by Calvinists. Alcott observed that children are playful by nature, having within themselves what they need to learn and grow, and are not empty vessels into which knowledge must be poured. If the child already has it within, the job of instructors is to facilitate the unfolding. As

Alcott's good friend and fellow educator William Russell stated, a truly human education should be based on the "great" principle that "every infant is already in possession of the faculties and apparatus required for his instruction." Since the child "uses these to a great extent himself" (by law of his constitution) the role of the teacher is "chiefly to facilitate this process of education, and to accompany the child in his progress, rather than to drive or even to lead him."[147]

While Bronson Alcott was open to influences, and well versed in the educational system developed by Johann Pestalozzi (1746–1827), he mostly relied on his own study of human nature and how to nurture it. This is apparent in a review of Pestalozzi's method that Alcott wrote for the 1829 *Journal of American Education*. After identifying who might have influenced Pestalozzi, Alcott noted that the Swiss educator may have come to these things on his own: "Whether he caught the ancient modes from the study of these great men's principles, or invented them anew, is not of so much moment as the truths by which his principles are governed." This is a perfect synopsis of Alcott himself. As a teenager and young man, he worked hard at self-improvement and read widely, gravitating toward material that connected with what he already perceived. His varied menu of Plato, Rousseau, the *Bhagavad Gita*, Coleridge, and John Bunyan's *Pilgrim's Progress* did not so much open up new vistas as reinforce his growing commitment to the divine goodness within each child. His meeting with Ralph Waldo Emerson only strengthened this vision.

In the latter half of the 1830s, Ralph Waldo Emerson provided a call to arms for the young American psyche. *Nature*, a small volume published in 1836, was a passionate invitation to the country to develop its own identity rather than rely on Europe. Emerson asked his readers, "Why should we not also enjoy an original relationship with the universe? Have our own poetry? Why should we grope among the dry bones of the past? The sun shines today also.... There are new lands, new men, new thoughts. Let us demand our own works and laws and worship."[148]

Emerson followed *Nature* with the "The American Scholar,"

---

147 From William Russell's review of "Essays on the Philosophy of Instruction..." in the 1829 *American Journal of Education*, p. 161.
148 Ralph Waldo Emerson in the Introduction to *Nature* (1836).

the *Phi Beta Kappa* address given at Harvard on August 31, 1837 and printed for distribution soon after. The charge to develop individual genius continued: "Meek young men grow up in libraries, believing it is their duty to accept the views which Cicero, which Locke, which Bacon have given, forgetful that Cicero, Locke, and Bacon were only young men in libraries when they wrote these books." Before long, the *Phi Beta Kappa* address was hailed as America's "Intellectual Declaration of Independence," inspiring many around him, including the extraordinary Peabody sisters of Salem, Massachusetts: Elizabeth, Mary, and Sophia.

Elizabeth Peabody, the eldest sister, was instrumental in a number of Transcendental undertakings, active in many reforms, and spearheaded the kindergarten movement in the United States. Middle sister Mary wed Horace Mann, the great advocate for public education and the first president of Antioch College. Sophia, the youngest, was an accomplished artist who married Nathaniel Hawthorne. Both Elizabeth and Sophia had been teaching assistants with Bronson Alcott at the Temple School, and both were close to Ralph Waldo Emerson.

One month before Sophia Peabody met her future husband, she devoured Emerson's *Phi Beta Kappa* address, and was filled with enthusiasm for the writer and his message. On October 1, 1837, she sat amidst the gravestones directly outside her home at 53 Charter Street in Salem and composed a lengthy letter to her brother George in New Orleans. Emerson, she wrote, keeps waking us up; he is our elder brother in spirit who, sitting in the "Tower of Thought," sees the vision of the new dawn with his "far reaching eye." We, the "sluggards," fold our hands and want more sleep, but Emerson "the Watchman" says, "No! No! The morning cometh."

What Emerson saw from the heights of his Tower was that every individual has a divine spark within and that it is every person's birthright to connect with the internal divine, without the need for a broker of any type. In the words of the most recent Emerson biographers, "Emerson's belief was that a god slumbers within the breast of every mechanic, farmer, engineer, poet, teacher — every human being. The process of awakening occurs first in thought as the Self becomes conscious of its own thinking and then seeks expression by shaping its surroundings according to its own thoughts."[149] As Emerson noted in a journal entry for April 7, 1840, "In all my lectures I have taught one doctrine, namely the infinitude of the private man."[150] By which he also means women.

The core principles of the "infinitude" of every person and of the "mind becoming aware of itself" were implicit in Sophia Peabody's description of the time her sister spent with both Emerson and the Unitarian minister, Frederick Hedge. Again to her brother George, she wrote, "Elizabeth has replenished her horn at the fountain of his [Emerson's] overflowing Dawn — You know her own is never empty. She has found out what she has herself, rather than received anything new, I suspect. Her faith in herself is freshened. I believe she never had such a splendid time in her life as she did last summer, first with Mr. Hedge & then with Mr. Emerson. One re-illumined her heart & the other her Reason. Long live both for making her so happy. She says she is going to lead an Emersonian life this winter..."[151]

Sophia captured the essence of Transcendental educational praxis: Elizabeth "has found out what she has herself, rather than received anything new." A worldview that presumes the innate worth of each individual is built upon the foundation that everyone comes into this world with inherent value. An educational system in harmony with this worldview would honor every student, understanding that in each child there is something of equal value to what lies in the teacher.[152]

Henry Thoreau was one who embraced the notion that a school should be a community of learners. After a brief teaching experience at age 20, Thoreau wrote to a mentor, "We should seek to be fellow students with the pupil, and should learn of, as well as with him, if we would be most helpful to him."[153] Thoreau realized at an

---

149 *Ralph Waldo Emerson: the Infinitude of the Private Man* (2008), Maurice York & Rick Spaulding, p. iv.
150 *The Journals of Ralph Waldo Emerson* edited by Edward W. Emerson, Houghton Mifflin, Boston, 1911, Vol. V, 1838–1841, pp. 380–381, April 7, 1840.
151 Sophia Peabody to George Peabody, October 1, 1837. Unpublished letter in the collection of the author.
152 *Cf* the statement of the Sant Bani School's founder, H.H. Kirpal Singh, *"Each one of us is unique in his own way. There is a divine purpose behind the life of everyone who comes into the world; no one has been created for nothing. We have something to learn from everyone. This is the mystery of humility."*
153 Henry David Thoreau to Orestes Brownson, December 30, 1837.

early age that individuals had access to different types of knowledge from sources other than ratiocination, which meant that "book-learnèd" instructors were not the sole keepers of the flame. As an adolescent, Thoreau had had a number of mystical experiences that were of "indescribable, infinite, all-absorbing, divine, heavenly pleasure, a sense of elevation and expansion," that left him "daily intoxicated... aloof from the society of men."[154] As he was transported outside of his normal consciousness, he sought help understanding the nature of these ecstatic times, but it was not until he discovered the sacred texts of the Asian Wisdom tradition that he fully grasped what had happened.[155] Thoreau understood, as Emerson had emphasized, that revelation was not a closed door, but open to all, including children. Access to this inner knowledge could be gained through meditative practices such as those outlined in the *Bhagavad Gita*, a favorite book of Thoreau, Emerson, and Alcott. The wisdom gained from this perspective put flesh on the spirits of the Wordsworthian beings that came into this world "trailing clouds of glory."

It is not that Thoreau, Emerson, and Alcott were teaching children how to access divine wisdom, but that they operated on the principle that each child had a noble center that unfolded best through encouragement and gentle guidance rather than through reconstruction. They recognized that each child was a meandering brook, sacred and free by nature, rather than a raw resource to be converted to a straight-cut ditch for societal ends. The Transcendental commitment to "the mind becoming aware of itself," to a classroom where children are taught to "talk about their thinking and feeling and reasoning," was a commitment to the core principle of honoring the essential value of the other as well as of your self (as that which is of value in you is also within me). The best example of this principle in action was the school at Brook Farm, the intentional community founded by the Transcendentalists.

In 1841, the Unitarian minister George Ripley resigned from

---

[154] Henry David Thoreau, Journal, July 16, 1851.

[155] For example, the *Sankhya Karika*, which Thoreau read in the Harvard Library, outlines the three ways of knowing: perception, inference, and revelation. See Sutra VI, *The Sankhya Karika or Memorial Verses on the Sankhya Philosophy by Iswara Krishna, translated by Henry Thomas Colebrooke combined with The Bhashya or Commentary of Guarapada, translated by Horace Hayman Wilson*, London, 1837.

his church and, with his wife Sophia and a small circle of friends, bought a farm in West Roxbury, Massachusetts, to create a model society built on the premise of equality for all. This most interesting experiment lasted until 1847, and attracted almost all of the brilliant minds of the day. Emerson, Thoreau, Alcott, Elizabeth Peabody, Nathaniel Hawthorne, and Margaret Fuller: all came to visit if they did not actually join. It was a lively environment for music, drama, the arts, philosophy, politics, and the spirit, as well as farming and industry, and was a sincere effort to bridge social and economic gaps.[156]

From the beginning, there were a number of good educators associated with Brook Farm, and the school they established on the land was successful financially as well as pedagogically. British social reformer Charles Lane[157] left a vivid account of the school at Brook Farm in the January 1842 edition of the Transcendentalist magazine, *The Dial*, in which he argues that the school "appears to present greater mental freedom than most other institutions." He describes the instruction as more "heart-rendered" and "heart-stirring," and concludes, "Brook Farm is a much improved model for the oft-praised schools of New England. It is time that the imitative and book-learned systems of the latter should be superseded or liberalized by some plan, better calculated to excite originality of thought, and the native energies of the mind.

A recent biographer of Brook Farm's co-founder, Sophia Ripley, provides more details on the experiential nature of the school. "The lessons in astronomy under the clear winter sky, the plays and masquerades in the woods, the Dante class in which Charles Dana and Mrs. Ripley and others read Dante in the original without an instructor, the trips into Boston to hear concerts of music by Beethoven, the singing of Mozart masses, the boat trips on the Charles River make Brook Farm sound like a school to dream about. For any child accustomed to the usual school of the 19th century it must

---

[156] For excellent recent studies of Brook Farm, see Sterling Delano, *Brook Farm: the Dark Side of Utopia* (2004); and Richard Francis, *Transcendental Utopias: Individual and Community at Brook Farm, Fruitlands, and Walden* (1997).

[157] Charles Lane was an austere social activist who accompanied Bronson Alcott back from England and helped him found the short-lived (June 1843 to January 1844) vegetarian community, Fruitlands, in Harvard, Massachusetts.

have been a wonderful experience."[158]

This is not a description of a straight-cut ditch, but of a school that honors the individual qualities of all members even as it celebrates practical and cultural achievements.

Thoreau's statement about ditches and brooks really does "just about say it all." The next time you are in front of a class, working hard to find and honor what is unique in each student, imagine the lineup of New England luminaries who are in your corner. Here are the Peabody sisters, the Ripleys, Bronson Alcott, Ralph Waldo Emerson, and, perhaps a little off by himself, Henry David Thoreau, all nodding and smiling in approval. Follow the course of that winding stream and you and your class may help create, in the words of Josiah Quincy, "the best thing attempted in modern times for a properly human culture."

---

[158] Henrietta Dana Raymond, *Sophia Willard Dana Ripley: Co-founder of Brook Farm* (1994), p. 39.

"The Asian Soul of Transcendentalism"[159]

The treatment of Transcendentalism by twentieth-century teachers of literature and American history has followed a long tradition of focusing primarily on the European and American cultural influences on its major figures, such as Ralph Waldo Emerson, Henry David Thoreau, Margaret Fuller, Elizabeth Peabody, and Bronson and Louisa May Alcott. Their work is seen as fitting into various Western currents such as German Romanticism, Unitarian theology, neo-Platonism, and American utopian thought. In this framework, their writings were of great significance, constituting the headwaters of Western environmentalism, Northern abolitionism, voting rights for women, advocacy of public education and curricular reform, inter-faith mysticism, and diet and health movements, among others.

To perceive the Transcendentalists as largely formed by and working in the Western intellectual tradition, however, is seriously flawed because it ignores a central strand in this cultural fabric: the influences from Asia. Despite the work of a few earlier scholars demonstrating the importance of Asian and Islamic traditions for the major Transcendentalists (e.g., Christy 1932), the Western-centered historical narrative still remains the focus in teaching about *Walden*, Emerson, and the writings of the Alcotts. It is time to reshape this too narrow and incorrect viewpoint and to understand that it was the Transcendentalists, among all Americans, who first gleaned the entire world of human religious belief and practice. As they relentlessly pursued "the universals" in human life, they assiduously borrowed and eagerly read the first translations of dozens of Asian and Islamic texts, acquiring their own copies whenever possible.

Recently, scholars such as Alan Hodder have expanded upon insights gleaned by earlier authors in demonstrating that Transcendentalism's leaders, Emerson and Thoreau, were seriously engaged in the reading of Asian religious texts as the first translations found

---

[159] Co-authored with Dr. Todd Lewis, Professor of World Religions at College of Holy Cross and published in the Fall 2011 issue of *Educating About Asia*, Vol. 16, No. 2, Association of Asian Studies, Ann Arbor, MI, pp. 12-18. Available on-line at http://aas2.asian-studies.org/EAA/EAA-Archives/16/2/978.pdf

their way into European languages, especially English.[160] As they creatively sought timeless transcultural spiritual truths, they were nourished by these first translations of the major works of Hinduism, Buddhism, Confucianism, Daoism, and Islam that were published in Europe.

Our view is that the Transcendentalists' enthusiasm and inspiration were founded on their realization that they were among the very first intellectuals to see the full global vision of human religious understanding. They realized that this spiritual knowledge from India, China, and Persia would open up a rich garden of new understandings, with the potential to alter human lives and civilization's destiny. Educator, writer, and father of novelist Louisa May Alcott, Bronson Alcott envisioned a "Bible of Mankind" that would capture the spiritual wisdom gathered from "Homer, Zoroaster, Vishnu, Gotama, Confucius, Mencius, Mahomet, mystics of the Middle Ages, and of times later."[161] Going beyond European and American ideas, the Transcendentalists absorbed fresh insights, reveled in the new realms of religious imagination, and sought ways of assimilating their global discoveries into a new world view that was in harmony with what they were seeing, perceiving, feeling, and experiencing.

Although the core "Transcendentalists" were amused by the name given to them by the public, they all believed that a Divine Essence enlivened everything and that this essence was available to every human being without the need of an intermediary. As Harvard professor and Emerson biographer Lawrence Buell observed about the Transcendentalists, "If you have to point to one and only one thing it would be the idea that Emerson expresses most powerfully, of the God or the Divine Principle within the individual self.... 'Every person has a spark of the divine.' Emerson wrote in his journal, 'I have been on the lecture circuit for a decade and I really have only one doctrine to preach: the infinitude of the private man.'"[162]

The most accessible way to experience the Divine Essence was

---

[160] Alan D. Hodder, *Thoreau's Ecstatic Witness* (New Haven: Yale University Press, 2001).

[161] Bronson Alcott, *Journals* II, (August 8, 1867), p. 388.

[162] Laura Knoy, "The American Transcendentalists: Essential Writings," New Hampshire Public Radio, Friday, April 7, 2006, interview with Lawrence Buell, http://www.nhpr.org/node/10499

through Nature, untrammeled by human hands, as this allowed for direct perception without first negotiating the sometimes narrow path of logical reasoning. As Emerson wrote in *Nature* (1836), the short text that was an open invitation to moving beyond the culture they inherited, "Why should we not also enjoy an original relationship with the universe? Have our own poetry? Why should we grope among the dry bones of the past? There are new lands, new men, new thoughts. Let us demand our own works and laws and worship."[163] The excitement these new discoveries engendered explains the vitality of the Transcendentalist movement.

Even in its 19th-century heyday, Transcendentalism never included more than a dozen major exponents, but it fostered enormously significant cultural initiatives, including two of America's utopian communities (Brook Farm and Fruitlands), an early women's rights manifesto (Fuller's *Woman in the Nineteenth Century*), influential moral discourses on the abolition of slavery, the nation's earliest influential voice of environmentalism (Thoreau's *Walden*), and a new style of travel writing (Fuller's *Summer on the Lakes*, Thoreau's *A Week on the Concord and Merrimack Rivers*, along with his travel narratives in Massachusetts, Maine, and Cape Cod). It is difficult to overstate the significance of Transcendentalism's richest and most original literature or how its leaders and their writings inspired new lineages of thought and a wealth of subsequent creative expression in each one of these fields.

What is now clear from studies of their journals and letters is how the Concord circle of Transcendentalists (Emerson, Thoreau, and Alcott) were all influenced in a deep and thoroughgoing way by the philosophies conveyed in Asian religious texts. Emerson eagerly sought out the newest publications from his Paris and London booksellers for their "revelations" drawn from "The East," and Thoreau revealed his excited consideration of their ideas in his journals and letters. While Thoreau had borrowed Asian texts from his good friend Emerson and the Harvard Library, in 1855 he received his own "nest of Indian books" — forty-four volumes in all — from a visiting Englishman who had made his acquaintance and understood his predilections. Thoreau, who could hardly believe his luck,

---

163 Ralph Waldo Emerson in the Introduction to *Nature* (1836).

built a special bookcase for these treasures that were, as he wrote to a friend, "in English, French, Latin, Greek, and Sanskrit." Calling them "a godsend," he eagerly shared the volumes with Emerson and Alcott.

Granted, authors of the books were often Europeans making first attempts to understand Asian traditions, and many of the works are full of terms, analogies, and conclusions that later scholars of these faiths would correct or reject. Nonetheless, in most cases, these works convey the essentials coherently enough for their learned American readers. For the Transcendentalists, this was no mere dabbling in the "exotic," as one school of earlier scholars had viewed their engagement in Asian texts. In the words of Arthur Christy, author of *The Orient in American Transcendentalism* and one of the first American academics to recognize the depth of this connection, the Transcendentalists turned to the scriptures of Asia because "they could not live with an absentee God."

Among the ancient texts read by Emerson, Thoreau and Alcott were *The Bhagavad Gita, The Vishnu Purana, The Upanishads, The Veda Samhitas, The Laws of Manu, The Samkhya Karika, The Dao Te Ching, The Analects of Confucius, The Heetopades of Veeshnoo-Sarma, The Harivamsa, Sakoontala by Kalidasa* and *The Megah Duta or Cloud Messenger.* The ideas the Transcendentalists found in this growing library of works from Hinduism, Buddhism, Confucianism, Daoism, and Sufism directly entered into their understanding of the world, shaped their vocations as writers, and informed their mission to disseminate the new intellectual and spiritual vistas these sages and saints were revealing. Although by now the scholarly evidence is well established that the Transcendentalists' engagement with Asian belief systems profoundly influenced their work, this important insight has not, for the most part, appeared in textbooks and popular treatment of this topic. It is our conviction that teachers who cover this movement and the writings of its major figures should highlight this Asian religions-Transcendentalism connection. This can be, in fact, a pivotal case study for classroom teaching about the globalization of cultural ideas. It can also be a case study of how the Euro-American ethnocentrism of scholars and teachers can limit understanding of even the greatest literary figures.

Part of the problem of seeing the Asian sources of Transcendentalism is that its chief figures did not spotlight them or readily use terms from these traditions in their most famous works. As much as they worked to deliver messages that awakened souls, the Transcendentalists also wanted what they wrote to be accessible and to sell. The result is that sources often lie buried. Similarly, one can easily move beyond the passing references to Hinduism in reading *Walden* to ponder the dense and rich evocations of the natural world that flow through this masterfully written text. Compare that to Thoreau's first book, *A Week on the Concord and Merrimack Rivers*, which — while laced with the wisdom of Confucius, the Buddha, the *Bhagavad Gita*, Hafiz, Dowlat Shah, and others — was a commercial failure. When Thoreau's Aunt Maria told him that all those references sounded like "blasphemy," and the influential critic James Russell Lowell complained, "We were bid to a river party, not to be preached at," Thoreau took it to heart.

While Emerson paid homage to these sources in poems like "Brahma" (below) and essays such as "The Oversoul" and "Persian Poetry," generally he did not emphasize the importance of these texts in his major published works. These authors were keen to reach as broad an audience as possible, not alienate their readers. There is little doubt that the writers (and their publishers) did not want what were then, in the general public, seen as esoteric, even bizarre ideas, to undermine the popularity of the works. Teachers and professors who have relied solely on the best-selling, canonical texts to form their understanding of the Transcendentalists are missing the rich source of Asian texts that so deeply informed the Concord group in particular and did much to shape their developing worldviews.

Brahma

If the red slayer think he slays,
Or if the slain think he is slain,
They know not well the subtle ways
I keep, and pass, and turn again.

Far or forgot to me is near;
Shadow and sunlight are the same;
The vanished gods to me appear;
And one to me are shame and fame.

They reckon ill who leave me out;
When me they fly, I am the wings;
I am the doubter and the doubt,
And I the hymn the Brahmin sings.

The strong gods pine for my abode,
And pine in vain the sacred Seven;
But thou, meek lover of the good!
Find me, and turn thy back on heaven.

The key to understanding and scaling the role of the Asian influences is found primarily in the journals they kept and the letters they wrote. The reading of *Walden* cannot miniaturize the inspiration of Asian religion once we know that Thoreau had a copy of *The Bhagavad Gita* on his bedside table in his cabin or once we read in his journal that the pond for him was "his Ganges River" where he retreated in the spirit of the ancient ascetic sages of India. Thoreau explicitly framed his entire "experiment" at Walden Pond, an extended metaphor for sounding the depths of the soul, as the ascetic practice of a Hindu *yogin*.

Thoreau's lifelong journal makes it clear that core Asian ideas powerfully transformed his intellectual and spiritual identity. In a journal entry of July 16, 1851, for example, Thoreau reflected on adolescent experiences of transcendent ecstasy that left him "daily intoxicated" with, "an indescribable, infinite, all-absorbing, divine, heavenly pleasure, a sense of elevation and expansion" that he had "nought to do with." He continued, "I speak as a witness on the stand, and tell what I have perceived. The morning and the evening were sweet to me, and I led a life aloof from the society of men." No one could explain these states to him, and it was not until he discovered sacred writings such as *The Upanishads* and *The Vishnu Purana* that the meaning of his experiences was put into a cogent spiritual context.

Thoreau's connection—to Hindu texts especially—bubble more to the surface in the travel accounts where he is more direct in acknowledging what was foremost in his mind at key moments. For example, Thoreau wrote in *A Week on the Concord and Merrimack Rivers*:

The reader is nowhere raised into and sustained in a higher, purer, or rarer region of thought than in The Bhagvat-Geeta . . . *The Oriental philosophy approaches, easily, loftier themes than the modern aspires to . . .* [assigning] *their due rank respectively to Action and Contemplation, or rather does full justice to the latter. Western philosophers have not conceived of the significance of Contemplation in their sense . . .*[164]

He goes on to describe people who have practiced the art of separating their mind from sensory perception and the depth of a new kind of knowledge that awaits such practices.

If Thoreau's writings and disposition incline toward the praxis of mysticism, Emerson dwells more in the realm of philosophy. As a young man, Emerson was encouraged by his spinster aunt, Mary Moody, to read Asian source texts. Fresh out of Harvard, he became a minister, only to discover that he found no sacredness in a ceremony like communion and therefore refused to offer it. He resigned from the Unitarian church, and, after his young wife died of tuberculosis, he found himself completely adrift. He sailed to Europe to meet some of the bright lights of the day, including William Wordsworth, Samuel Taylor Coleridge, and Thomas Carlyle. While looking at a large exhibition of plants and animals in Paris — arranged in such a way as to highlight incremental growth as well as connectivity — Emerson was struck by the fact that all life is part of a web and that change is the constant state in which life finds itself. This existential insight enlivened his mind, and he never looked back: it was in Asian texts that Emerson found particularly rich images of life's fundamental inner-connectivity. He continually read a wide range of texts in search of what he called "lusters" — pearls of wisdom that would inform his ever-expanding worldview. As his first biographer, James Elliot Cabot, noted while describing Emerson's reading preferences, "The Oriental (particularly the Hindoo) religious books, *The Bhagavat Gita, The Puranas,* and *Upanishads* were among his favorites." These books, according to Emerson,

---

[164] Henry David Thoreau, *A Week on the Concord and Merrimack Rivers* (New York: Charles Scribner's Sons, 1849), p. 110. This work is available online, digitized by Google, at http://tinyurl.com/67u7kuq.

...are for the scholar's idle times. When he can read God directly, the hour is too precious to be wasted in other men's transcripts of their readings. But when the intervals of darkness come, as come they must — when the sun is hid, and the stars withdraw their shining — we repair to the lamps which were kindled by their ray, to guide our steps to the East again, where the dawn is.[165]

Whereas Thoreau relied on these texts to validate his own ecstatic experiences, Emerson plucked jewels from wherever he found them to underscore his philosophic belief in "the infinitude of the private man," for as he wrote, "I believe in Eternity. I can find Greece, Asia, Italy, Spain, and the Islands — the genius and creative principle of each and of all eras in my own mind."[166]

Transcendentalism and the Global Dialectic

The influence of the Transcendentalists was profound and continues to be so. By the late nineteenth century, many in New England were interested enough in "Eastern thought" that journeys to India were not uncommon. Reverend Phillip Brooks, the highly popular minister of Concord's Trinity Church, wrote his sister-in-law from India that a pilgrimage to the tree where the Buddha found enlightenment was now a "duty of a minister who preaches to Bostonians."[167] When asked about her religious beliefs in 1884, well-known novelist Louisa May Alcott wrote:

The simple Buddha religion is very attractive to me, and I believe in it. God is enough for me and all the prophets are only stepping stones to him... I seem to remember former states before this...[168]

Bronson Alcott, Louisa's father, was intimately involved in the publication of the book that brought the Buddha's life more into American consciousness than any text before: Edwin Arnold's *The*

---

[165] Ralph Waldo Emerson, "The American Scholar," 1837.
[166] *The Essays of Emerson, Volume the First,* "History," 1899, London: Arthur L. Humphreys, p. 9.
[167] Carl T. Jackson, *The Oriental Religions and American Thought: Nineteenth-Century Explorations* (Santa Barbara, CA: Greenwood Publishing Group, 1982), p. 141.
[168] Louisa May Alcott, Letter to Maggie Lukens, February 5, 1884.

Light of Asia sold over half a million copies in Europe and America. The work of the Concord Summer School of Philosophy, with its lectures on Asian texts, amongst many other topics, was carried further in the late 1800s and early 1900s by intrepid Bostonians like Sara Chapman Bull. It was Swami Vivekananda's connections with women, such as Bull and others in Boston, that opened the doors wide for him at the Chicago World Parliament of Religions in 1893, and the time he spent in Massachusetts, Maine, and New York gave birth to the first Vedanta Centers in the US.

The ripple effect of interest in Asian texts continued decades after the decline of Transcendentalism. Henry Salt, the extraordinary British socialist, was so taken by the writings of Thoreau that he wrote perhaps the best early biography of him. Salt was active in animal rights and dietary reform — and it was Salt's pamphlet on vegetarianism that gave a young student of law in London, Mohandas K. Gandhi, the strength not to succumb to the voices around him that were insisting that he change his diet. Later in life, Gandhi wrote to Salt about diet and the influence of Thoreau:

> Camp Hardoi
> October 12th, 1929

> *Dear friend,*
>
> *I was agreeably surprised to receive your letter. Yes, indeed your book which was the first English book I came across on vegetarianism was of immense help to me in steadying my faith in vegetarianism.*
>
> *My first introduction to Thoreau's writings was I think in 1907 or later when I was in the thick of the passive resistance struggle. A friend sent me Thoreau's essay on civil disobedience. It left a deep impression upon me. I translated a portion of that essay for the readers of Indian Opinion in South Africa which I was then editing and I made copious extracts from that essay for the English part of that paper.*
>
> *That essay seemed to be so convincing and truthful that I felt the need of knowing more of Thoreau and I came across your life of him, his "Walden" and other short essays all of which I read with great pleasure and equal profit.*
>
> *Yours sincerely,*
> *M.K. Gandhi*

In the 1960s, the praxis of the Civil Rights Movement, as developed by Martin Luther King, Jr., derived much inspiration from the teachings of Gandhi—and in turn from the writings of Thoreau, particularly the essay "Resistance to Civil Government," or, as it is now known, "Civil Disobedience." The stature of both Thoreau and Emerson continues to grow, and several recent studies have examined the educational philosophies of Alcott (and Thoreau), shedding light on their holistic approach in the classroom. At play in the field of all of the above were the teachings of the classic Asian religious texts.

Conclusion

Transcendentalism represents an important moment in a new American consolidation of global religious awareness. Seeing such strong connections that were so pervasive in one of America's most original intellectual movements—and with *Walden* long-installed as part of the Western canon—now is the time to understand and teach this intellectual movement as a watershed moment, one in which influential American thinkers began to conceptualize a world where Asia and the West met, and the full spectrum of humanity's spiritual understandings were creatively synthesized. Their pioneering curiosity for exploring other peoples' literatures, philosophies, and spirituality is no less important or relevant for our own time.

Bibliography

Bosco, Ronald, Joel Myerson, Daisaku Ikeda. *Creating Waldens: An East-West Conversation on the American Renaissance* (Cambridge: Dialogue Path Press, 2009).

Buell, Lawrence, ed. *The American Transcendentalists: Essential Writings* (NY: Modern Library Classics, 2006).

Carpenter, Frederic Ives. *Emerson and Asia* (Harvard University Press, 1931).

Ch'en, David T.Y. "Thoreau and Taoism" in C.D. Narasimhaiah, ed. *Asian Response to American Literature* (Delhi: Vikas, 1972) 406-16.

Christy, Arthur. *The Orient In American Transcendentalism: A Study Of Emerson, Thoreau, And Alcott* (New York: Columbia University Press, 1932).

Clarke, J. J. *Oriental Enlightenment: the Encounter Between Asian and Western Thought* (New York: Routledge, 1997).

Fields, Rick. *How the Swans Came to the Lake: A Narrative History of Buddhism in America* (Boulder: Shambhala 1981).

Francis, Richard. *Fruitlands: The Alcott Family and Their Search for Utopia.* (New Haven: Yale University Press, 2010.

Goldberg, Philip. *American Veda: From Emerson and the Beatles to Yoga and Meditation: How Indian Spirituality Changed the West* (NY: Harmony, 2010).

Gura, Philip F. *American Transcendentalism: A History* (NY: Hill and Wang, 2008).

Hodder, Alan D. *Thoreau's Ecstatic Witness* (New Haven: Yale University Press, 2001).

_____ "Concord Orientalism, Thoreauvian Autobiography, and the Artist of Kouroo," in Charles Capper and Conrad Wright, eds. *Transient and Permanent: The Transcendentalist Movement and Its Contexts*, (Boston: Massachusetts Historical Society, 1999), 190-226.

_____ "Ex Oriente Lux": Thoreau's Ecstasies and the Hindu Texts," *The Harvard Theological Review*, 86 (4), 1993, pp. 403-438.

Jackson, Carl T. *The Oriental Religions and American Thought: Nineteenth Century Explorations* (Greenwood Press, 1982).

Jeswine, Miriam Alice. "Henry David Thoreau: Apprentice to the Hindu Sages" (Doctoral Dissertation, University of Oregon, 1971).

MacIver, Roderick, ed. *Thoreau and the Art of Life: Precepts and Principles.* (Ferrisberg, Vt: Heron Dance, 2006).

Matteson, John. *Eden's Outcasts: The Story of Louisa May Alcott and Her Father* (W.W. Norton, 2008).

Myerson, Joel, ed. *Transcendentalism: A Reader.* (New York: Oxford University Press, 2000).

Narayan, Kirin. "Refractions of the Field at Home: American Representations of Hindu Holy Men in the 19th and 20th Centuries," *Cultural Anthropology* 8 (4), 1993, pp. 476-509.

Oldmeadow, Harry. *Journeys East: 20th Century Western Encounters with Eastern Religious Traditions* (Bloomington: World Wisdom, 2004).

Patri, Umesh. *Hindu Scriptures and American Transcendentalists.* (Delhi: Intellectual Book Corner, 1998).

Prabuddha Pravrajika. *Saint Sara: The Life of Sara Chapman Bull, the American Mother of Swami Vivekanada* (Calcutta: Shri Sarada Math, 2002).

Qian, Mansu. *Emerson and China – Reflections on Individualism* (cited in Bureau of International Cooperation, Hong Kong, Maco and Taiwan Academic Affairs Office Chinese Academy of Social Sciences 2003.3.10).

Rayapati, J P Rao. *Early American Interest in Vedanta* (Calcutta: Asia Publishing House, 1973).

Reynolds, Larry J. "The Cimeter's 'Sweet' Edge: Thoreau, Contemplation, and Violence," *Nineteenth Century Prose,* Volume 31 (2), 2004, 121-148.

Riepe, Dale. "Emerson and Indian Philosophy," *Journal of the History of Ideas* 28, 1967, 11-22.

Rosa, Alfreda F. "Charles Ives: Music, Transcendentalism, and Politics," *The New England Quarterly* 44 (3), 1971, 433-443.

Schmidt, Lee. *Restless Souls: The Making of American Spirituality, from Emerson to Oprah* (New York: Harper One, 2005).

Schwab, Raymond. *The Oriental Renaissance: Europe's Rediscovery of India and the East 1680-1880.* (New York: Columbia University Press, 1987).

Scott, David. "Rewalking Thoreau and Asia: 'Light from the East' for 'A Very Yankee Sort of Oriental'" *Philosophy East and West,* 57 (1), 2007), p. 14-39.

Stein, William, ed. *Two Brahman Sources of Emerson and Thoreau* (Gainesville, Fla: Scholars Facsimiles and Reprints, 1967).

Syman, Stefanie. *The Subtle Body: The Story of Yoga in America* (NY: Farrar-Straus, 2010).

Takanashi, Yoshio. "Emerson and Zhu Xi: The Role of the 'Scholar' in Pursuing 'Peace,'" *The Japanese Journal of American Studies,* No. 20, 2009, 1-31.

Tweed, Thomas A. "The Seeming Anomaly of Buddhist Negation": American Encounters with Buddhist Distinctiveness, 1858-1877," *The Harvard Theological Review,* Vol. 83 (1), 1990, 65-92.

Versluis, Arthur. *American Transcendentalism & Asian Religions* (Oxford Univ. Press, 1993).

Williamson, Lola. *Transcendent in America: Hindu-Inspired Meditation Movements as New Religion* (NYU Press, 2010).

About the Author

Kent Bicknell grew up in central New Hampshire and resides there still. His spiritual quest culminated in receiving initiation in 1968 from Master Kirpal Singh (1894-1974) of New Delhi, India. In 1976 he came close to Sant Ajaib Singh (1926-1997) of Rajasthan, India. After more than twenty-five visits to India as well as traveling extensively in Central and South America with Sant Ji, he published *Rainbow On My Heart: A Memoir of the Early Years of the Mission of Sant Ajaib Singh* (2002).

In 1973 Kent became founding head of Sant Bani School (www.santbani.org) and stayed as a teaching head for 44 years, retiring in 2017. He was a Scholar of the House at Yale University, and holds a master's degree from Goddard College and a doctorate in curriculum development from Boston University. Kent has been involved in education for five decades, including over forty years on the Advisory Council of the New Hampshire Commissioner of Education and six years as a commissioner with the New England Association of Schools and Colleges. He has served as a consultant to schools across the U.S. as well as in Bhutan, Canada, Colombia, Guatemala, India and Venezuela

An independent scholar whose work has been published in a variety of journals, Kent's main interests are the New England Transcendentalists: Henry David Thoreau, Ralph Waldo Emerson, and the Alcott Family; their educational pedagogy and how they were inspired by the spiritual traditions of Asia. In 1995, he acquired, edited and published the manuscript of *A Long Fatal Love Chase*, a gothic thriller by Louisa May Alcott that became a New York Times best seller.

Made in the USA
Lexington, KY
28 October 2019